FRENCH FILM

THE NATIONAL CINEMA SERIES
General Editor: ROGER MANVELL

★

SOVIET CINEMA
Thorold Dickinson and Catherine de la Roche

THE ITALIAN CINEMA
Vernon Jarratt

SCANDINAVIAN FILM
Forsyth Hardy

FRENCH FILM

BY

GEORGES SADOUL

THE FALCON PRESS

First published in 1953
by the Falcon Press (London) Limited
6 & 7 Crown Passage, Pall Mall London, S W I
Printed in Great Britain
by The Alcuin Press, Welwyn Garden City, Herts
Copyright 1953 by Georges Sadoul

CONTENTS

FOREWORD

NO country has contributed more than France to the art of the film. During the nineteen-thirties the better French films shown in Britain became the subject of an adulation by the intelligentsia which, though it was partly based on intellectual snobbery, showed also that certain French film-makers had learnt how to give their art a humanity, a subtlety of treatment and a maturity which was uncommon in the work of the period.

Georges Sadoul is a prolific writer on the cinema. During the war years he began work on the *Histoire Générale du Cinéma*, which from its initial volume, published in 1946, established his reputation as an outstanding historian of the film, and which, in 1952, reached its fourth volume. No one could be better qualified to write for British readers this present record and evaluation of the French cinema.

It has become a tradition to dedicate the individual book in this series to the film-makers and film critics of the country which forms the subject of each volume. France has contributed as much to film criticism as she has to film-making, and we are glad to pay the tribute of this book to a country from which we have gained so much.

ROGER MANVELL

I

THE PIONEERS:
LUMIÈRE, MÉLIÈS, ZECCA

1890–1908

IN October 1888, at the Académie des Sciences in Paris, Jules Marey first demonstrated his moving pictures. These he had recorded with his chronophotographe as a strip of photographs, each showing the stage of a movement slightly more advanced than the one before, which, when projected, showed a picture, alive and moving. In the following years, Marey and his assistant, Demeny, successfully recorded many similar strips of photographic images on paper, and eventually on celluloid. And then they progressed to the stage when, in 1892, Demeny projected in public the animated close-ups of a figure actually pronouncing such brief phrases as 'Je vous aime' and 'Vive la France'.

During this time, Emile Reynaud, a craftsman of genius, had been constructing an Optique Théâtre, which he patented and displayed at the Paris World Exhibition of 1889. This apparatus, very similar to Marey's, was designed to project an unwinding, perforated strip of animated drawings, but was unlike that of Marey who continued to use photographs. By 1890 Reynaud had already completed several 'films' for the Theatre Optic; *Clown et ses Chiens* and *Un Bon Bock*. These two films were shown at the Grevin Museum, the French equivalent to Madame Tussaud's, in 1892. Reynaud, a prodigious worker, maintained an astonishing output of such 'cartoons', of invention and colour; *Pauvre Pierrot*, *Autour d'une Cabine*, *Rêve au Coin du Feu*. These were the first of their sort to be made and the first to be publicly shown; they

1

created a great demand and established a vogue that lasted until the turn of the century.

So it is primarily due to the pioneer work of Jules Marey and his chronophotographe, followed by Reynaud with his Optic Theatre that France was able to celebrate her sixtieth anniversary of cinema in 1950.

The infant cinema was five years old when Louis Lumière gave it an impetus, powerful both commercially and industrially, by producing with his now famous cinématograph the first real moving photographs. Amongst the audience at the first screening of Lumière's films sat a certain Georges Méliès, director of the Robert Houdin Theatre. This first encounter between Lumière, the inventor of moving photographs, and Méliès, the future creator of the *mise-en scène*, was of great significance. The individual contribution of these two men provided the roots from which cinematographic art throughout the world has since grown. Moving pictures offered Lumière an opportunity that he was not slow to grasp—at the time it was said, 'Il saisit la nature sur le vif'. As leading manufacturer of photographic equipment, he had already made a fortune out of amateur photography. His early films were in subject, as in technique, amateur animated photographs. Lumière turned his camera, the camera he had invented and which had been constructed for him by the engineer Carpentier, on to the most familiar, everyday subjects; the city street, the bathing beach, marching soldiers, a railway station, a public garden. In making these films he called upon all the skill he had developed with the still camera, resourcefully framing his subjects, using angle shots, and making the most of light and shade.

Up to the year 1895, Lumière produced: *La Sortie des Usines*, *Le Déjeuner de Bébé*, *La Sortie du Port*, *La Démolition d'un Mur*, *L'Arrivée du Train en Gare*, *La Partie d'Écarté*. In all these short seventeen-metre films, Lumière's approach to the subject was simple and direct, equally direct was his processing equipment at this period—these films he developed himself at home in an ordinary bucket. The public, seeing these films, identified themselves with the people on the screen and, thanks to Lumière, came to understand that from this new machine they could expect something more than a mere illusion, unlike Edison's Kinetoscope.

Louis Lumière created his own kind of treatment of familiar, everyday objects, *scène de genre*. Throughout his fifty odd films there runs a

2

probably unintentional portrayal of the life, the pleasures and the pastimes of the French *bourgeoisie* at the turn of the century. These films paved the way to other kinds of treatment.

The innovations of Lumière did not end here. By filming the French Photographic Society's Congress he found himself the originator of newsreels. His famous *Arroseur-Arrosé* contained the first suggestion of the gag and the comic film. And the group of four films he made around the *Pompiers de Lyon*, *Sortie de la Pompe*, *Mise en Batterie*, *L'Attaque du Feu* and *Le Sauvetage* was the first documentary. This four-part film also showed an advance in technique, consisting of a series of shots taken at different times in different places. Montage, or the process of editing, had made its first appearance, indicating the way in which cinematic narrative could be constructed. With this development, the history of the cinema begins to take on a more complex form.

Early in 1896, Louis Lumière recruited a score or so of enthusiastic assistants. These he trained and sent around the world to screen his films, shooting fresh material as they went. How successful the cinematograph proved is now common knowledge, together with the initial superiority of Lumière's enterprises to those of his rivals (such as Edison, R. W. Paul or Skladanowski) in other countries. And as if in tribute to this successful pioneer, the word 'cinematograph', or abbreviations and variants like Cine, Cinema, Kine and Kinema were used to denote this new form of entertainment. Lumière was soon amply rewarded for his initiative. For nearly two years he had crowds from the five continents, from Spain to Africa, from Sweden to the States, from Mexico to Japan, rushing to his screenings.

The stroke of genius which prompted Lumière to train his assistants to be camera-men as well as projectionists was to bear rich rewards. With increasing practical experience came the invention of new techniques. In the spring of 1896, Promio, for example, while in Venice, rigged his camera on a gondola gliding down the Grand Canal, thus originating travelling or 'panning' shots as we call them to-day. At the same time Perrigot and Doublier in Moscow made the first great newsreel scoop with seventeen shots of the coronation of Tsar Nicolas II. A short time after, a 400-metre film was devoted entirely to one subject—the famous Military School of Cavalry at Saumur—by an unnamed director. And while in 1897 Georges Hatot was directing for Clement Maurice a few short comic sketches staged on rudimentary sets, yet

3

another Lumière trainee was shooting, rather clumsily, a passion play at Horitz in Bohemia.

The time came for Lumière to tighten the rein on his rapidly developing school. A definite trend towards *mise-en-scène*—stagecraft—was developing, and as a manufacturer of photographic equipment he had no wish to encourage this form of theatre. So the progressive work of his followers was checked; Lumière was content with his achievement as the creator of the newsreel and of the documentary as distinct from the scientific film, this having been previously invented by the physiologist, Jules Marey.

*   *   *

'Georges Méliès set the cinema along the path towards theatrical spectacle, and introduced the extravagant costume film, imposing décor, historical reconstructions, drama, comedies, opera, etc.' These words were written by Georges Méliès himself in his autobiography. He goes on, 'In the development of the cinema I have played a more important part than Lumière. The industrial success of the invention is primarily due to those who have utilized the film to exhibit their personal productions. . . . At all times I have endeavoured to develop the industry as a whole, and to create a considerable part of its technical processes.'

Under the influence of Méliès the cinema ceased to be 'merely a machine for reproducing life'; it became an art. When he stumbled across the cinema, this son of a wealthy Paris manufacturer had been following various callings, first a draughtsman, then conjurer. For the past ten years he had been directing a small theatre specializing in conjuring, founded by Robert Houdin.

Méliès, the man of the theatre, nevertheless went into the open air to shoot his first films; these early efforts were often made in close association with Lumière, who to his dying day referred to Méliès as the man who stole his ideas. These pictures, under the trade name of Star Film, enjoyed such financial success that by 1897, Méliès was able to build the world's first film studio. Under the name of Atelier de Poses it consisted of a large photographic studio with glass walls and roof and with a movable stage on which the different sets were built. This now-famous studio was built in the garden of his Montreuil estate, setting the pattern for film studios throughout the world; it was still in use thirty

4

years later and was only rendered obsolete by the advent of talking films.

Méliès excelled in films of fantasy. His inspiration sprang from the popular Paris plays of the day showing in theatres such as the Chatelet and from literary sources—Perrault's fairy tales, nursery rhymes, the books of Jules Verne and H. G. Wells. The English music-halls immediately absorbed all his output, becoming his best clients, soon to be followed by the United States; Anglo-Saxon folk-lore strongly influenced his productions of this period.

Among his successful fantasies, the chief are *Cinderella* (1899), *The Christmas Dream* (1900), *Red Riding Hood* and *Blue Beard* (1901)—*A Trip to the Moon* (1902), *Fairyland, or the Kingdom of the Fairies* and *The Damnation of Faust* (1903), *An Impossible Voyage*, *The Christmas Angels* and *The Palace of the Arabian Nights* (1904), *The Chimney Sweep*, *The Merry Frolics of Satan* and *The Witch* (1906), *Under the Seas* and *The Eclipse* (1907) and *À La Conquête du Pôle* (1912). In the making of all these pictures, the length of which averaged some thousand feet, Méliès not only directed the cast, including crowds of extras, sometimes 200 or 300 strong, but wrote the script, designed the sets, selected the costumes and also acted in the star roles. In addition, he himself invented, perfected and maintained all the 'trick' devices essential to his fantasy films.

For his 'tricks' Méliès used all those known in the world of theatre (long-tried stage devices such as trap-doors, changes of scene and flying effects). But his principal contribution to screen technique was the adaptation of many special effects already used in still photography, such as superimposition, double or multiple exposure, and the dissolve. His technical skill and ingenuity knew no bounds, and it is thanks to his experiments that the modern technique of film-making has been built up.

In other respects, however, Méliès' technique lagged behind that of Lumière. His new studio kept him prisoner and he soon lost the stimulus of overcoming difficulties and the freedom of working in the open-air. Lumière and his colleagues, on the other hand, unshackled by the confines of a studio, tore away all the old stage conventions, and so laid the foundations of modern cinema technique as we know it to-day. It was these pioneers who liberated the camera from its static position in front of the stage, and it was they who introduced all kinds of angle shots, panning and elementary montage. When Méliès heard about these revolutionary methods, he dismissed them with contempt as being too unorthodox for his consideration.

5

It was Méliès' habit to divide his productions into scenes or tableaux, and the audience were expected to view them as if seated in the front stalls of the theatre. The actors were accordingly placed on the stage, surrounded by the conventional 'wings', friezes and a broadly painted backcloth. To complete the illusion of an actual theatre, Méliès even arranged for the credits and titles to appear, as if on a stage curtain, and brought back the cast to bow to the applause anticipated at the end of the film. It was the chief merit of Méliès that he explored every device of the theatre in order to exploit it for the cinema, but he ultimately became and remained a slave to the most rigid of theatrical conventions. On the other hand, the technique he adopted did allow him, paradoxically, great creative freedom in the world of fantasy: often from his prolific and beguiling imagination there flows an intense poetry. This world of Méliès, a synthetic world with its own wilful, arbitrary laws, is closely akin, notwithstanding all its naïve lightheartedness, to that darker world of German expressionism.

Even though he turned a blind eye to 'life', it would be wrong to say that Méliès ignored reality. Side by side with his fairy tales, he worked in another style—a re-enactment of history. With all the reality of a newsreel he reconstructed events of recent history. Using screen sets and professional actors, with meticulous care and research, Méliès succeeded in representing reality in films like *L'Explosion du Cuirassé Maine* (1898), *La Guerre Greco-Turque* and *L'Affaire Dreyfus* (1899), *Les Incendiares* and *Le Couronnement du Roi Edouard VII* (1902). These productions were preceded by scrupulous documentation, the director trying to imitate the 'on-the-spot' effect of actual newsreels. In the case of *Le Couronnement du Roi Edouard VII* he built his sets from authentic photographs; eye-witness technical advisers were consulted and the original master-of-ceremonies was brought over from London to assist in the production and supervision of the details. In his various writings, Méliès lays great stress on the 'realism' of these settings—a realism to be found also in certain parts of his fantasies (like *The Chimney Sweep* or *Under the Seas*). With these somewhat naïvely-inspired reconstructions he was, without realizing it, pointing the way for the documentary film movement, which was later to record actual events as and where they happened, away from the studios and without professional actors.

Georges Méliès was without doubt a true craftsman. He was his own producer and his own exhibitor, and this absorbing interest in the cinema lost him the major part of his large private fortune. Méliès was an individualist, and inspired few genuine followers in his way of film-making. Nevertheless, he had countless imitators in France as well as in all the other countries where the cinema was developing after 1900. His influence was at its height in the early years of the new century. His two great innovations, the *mise-en-scène* and the film story, were by then generally regarded as essential elements of the cinema, and it was thanks to Méliès that films were already attracting huge crowds to every enter-prising fairground that boasted a 'canvas palace' for the projection of the new moving pictures.

To this fairground public of 1901 came the Pathé Brothers firm. This company, founded by Charles Pathé and known in France as Pathé Frères, richly backed by French banks and the financial resources of heavy industries, had for some years been manufacturing and whole-saling phonographs and phonograph cylinders. They first started film-making as a side-line activity, and emphasis was placed on films of crime and on love stories—the directors of the firm having grasped long before Hollywood that sex and shooting were destined to be the pillars of box-office attraction. The production of Pathé films was sporadic, however, until 1901 when Charles Pathé entrusted the direction of their new studios at Vincennes to a former music-hall singer, Ferdinand Zecca.

Like Méliès before him, Zecca began by plagiarizing. His most immediate source of inspiration was the British film, and, in imitating the work of G. A. Smith, James Williamson and William Paul, he learned how to modify and adapt the over-rigid conventions of the Méliès technique—at the same time as he was 'borrowing' from the work of Méliès himself. The British directors, especially those of the Brighton School, had broken away from Lumière and evolved a new technique of their own. Long before Griffith came along they began using for the first time a planned montage, and such technical innova-tions as close-ups and the development of parallel action. These tech-niques were freely borrowed by Zecca, who continued imitating them until he developed his own original contribution by experiment. It was Zecca who was mainly instrumental in freeing the cinema from the theatrical prison house built up around it by Méliès. Ferdinand Zecca's contribution was less important in technique than in subject matter. He had a receptive ear for the demands of his fairground public and he studied the reports sent in by Pathé representatives from all parts of the world where a huge organization was rapidly growing. Pathé profits at this time were pouring in by millions of francs at a time; during some years dividends were paid out which were many times greater than the invested capital. This huge success was largely due to Zecca's responsiveness to the needs of the crowds, and his pandering to public taste by exploiting scandals, best-selling novelettes and other sensational material as themes for his productions. Audiences, whose appetites for this sort of fare were being whetted by the innovation of the big, mass-circulation journals, were delighted.

Zecca's first great successes were *Les Victimes de l'Alcool* and *L'Histoire d'un Crime* (1901–2), stories of the 'lower classes', the poverty-stricken and criminals of the underworld. They initiated the catalogue of the Pathé film series of dramatic and realistic films, to which Zecca soon added *Au Pays Noir* and *La Grève*. Although these were melodramas meant to appeal to suburbia, the influence of Zola's literary naturalism can be seen in them, in particular that of *Germinal* and *L'Assommoir*. Yet another of Zecca's great successes was the *Passion de Notre Seigneur Jésus-Christ*, 2,000 feet in length, made over the period 1902–5, in a style directly inspired by the popular chromo-lithographs of the period on sale in all the bookshops. Zecca's technique at this time, although still rudimentary, represents in some respects an advance on that of Méliès (in the use of the 'panning-shot', for example, shooting with a continuously moving camera across the studio); in brief, he freed the camera from its old rooted spot in front of the stage. Other traditional subjects (like William Tell, Don Quixote and Samson) were made by Pathé and directed by Zecca, or by other of the firm's directors, in some cases by men originally in charge of recruiting and directing crowd players—Georges Hatot, Lucien Nonguet, Lépine, Gaston Velle, Louis Gasnier, André Heuzé, Georges Monca and Albert Capellani—these became known collectively as the Vincennes School. Among the productions made by this group were a number of fantasies, following less the traditions of Méliès than that of the Théâtre du Châtelet, *La Poule aux Oeufs d'Or*, *Voyage Autour d'Une Étoile* and *L'Amant de la Lune*. The most successful specialist in this genre was Georges Velle. But perhaps of all Pathé films, it was the comedies that won the greatest success, with basic elements in the presentation consisting of the 'gag', the trick shot, and, of course, the chase—this last an importation from Britain, particularly from the Clarendon films.

8

Pathé Brothers considered themselves to be supreme, and anonymity shrouded their personnel. Players, script-writers, directors and stage designers were unknown to the public. They were either on the permanent pay-roll, or signed up from film to film, and all were equally poorly paid. Legitimate stage actors were at that time ashamed to appear in films; there were, however, a few comedians, who, hiding their real identities under pseudonyms, achieved a rapid success with the general public. The first of these was André Deed, known successively as Boireau, Gribouille and Cretinetti; he was followed and soon supplanted by Max Linder and Prince Rigadin.

For the first ten years of the twentieth century, the Pathé dramas and then the comedies and realistic films dominated the world market (at this time films were sold outright, not rented as they are to-day). The sale of all these Pathé films went into hundreds and sometimes thousands of copies, bringing in profits fifty or a hundred times the cost of their production. With agents established in every quarter of the globe, it was not long before Pathé film production started in countries such as Italy, Great Britain, America, Russia, Germany and Japan. With such wide ramifications, it is not surprising that the firm of Pathé Brothers in 1908 sold twice as many films in the United States as all the American producing companies put together.

II

THE FILMS D'ART, COMEDIES
DETECTIVE SERIALS

1908–1914

MEANWHILE, changes were taking place in the presentation of films. The fairground tent of early days was giving way to small halls in the suburbs and theatres on the boulevards. Charles Pathé copied the English idea of building a network of picture 'palaces' throughout the country. Further, he put a sudden stop to the accepted practice of selling his films outright, and initiated the system of hiring out the sole rights of exhibiting (1907). Pathé also realized that the cinema only drew a small percentage of possible audiences; he wished to attract the theatre-going habitués as well. Six years before America, the French cinema realized that its next step was to call upon established actors of repute to appear in famous plays—and he prevailed upon the Académie Française and Comédie Française to lend their support. In exploring the possibilities of a new type of film, the 'film d'art' was born. The first of this more select kind of film was *L'Assassinat du duc de Guise*, 1908, which immediately set the seal of success upon the venture. This film was produced by Le Film d'Art, a new group inaugurated by Lafitte, the financier, and part controlled by Pathé. *Le Duc de Guise* was directed by Le Bargy, an illustrious actor from the Comédie Française, who also took the principal role: his assistant director was André Calmettes, a fellow-actor, and the cast was composed of their colleagues from the Comédie, Albert Lambert, Huguette Duflos, Berthe Bovy, and others. The script was the work of an Académician, Henri Lavedan,

10

and the music was specially composed by Camille Saint-Saëns.

Prior to the *Duc de Guise*, French films consisted mainly of a series of living tableaux with plenty of stage effects and chases, but the actors were merely swaying silhouettes, like forms in a silent ballet. Le Bargy was the first to attempt in film the presentation of a character of real psychological interest and verisimilitude, and the expression of complex sentiments. This was an important innovation, which D. W. Griffith, even twenty years later, considered as new, bold and revolutionary.

The Society of the Film d'Art brought its first love, the theatre, with it and all too easily fell into the set clichés first perpetrated by Méliès: its films were theatre in celluloid, every scene was shot straight through, from the same camera position, and simply presented the resulting series of images with no attempt to edit sequences.

If Italy, Great Britain, Denmark, Germany and eventually America were deeply influenced by the experiments of the Film d'Art, France herself was less impressed and still content to use only second-class players, stock stage plays, and scripts carelessly dashed off by indifferent writers. Nevertheless, a few films of some real quality did emerge— such films as *Notre Dame de Paris*, *Les Mystères de Paris*, *Les Misérables* (all made by Albert Capellani for Pathé); *Madame Sans Gêne*, with the great actress Réjane and perhaps the most outstanding of all, *La Reine Elisabeth*, made in a London studio by Desfontaines and Mercanton, directing the renowned Sarah Bernhardt, who also appeared in *La Dame Aux Camélias*.

For the greater part, however, mediocrity prevailed as the unfortunate rule; these few films were the exception. Following the peak period of 1908, the French cinema, resting too comfortably on the laurels of its now firmly established industrial superiority, showed no inclination for the artistic experimentation that could alone preserve its vitality. After reaching a certain peak, stagnation, and then inevitable decline set in, hastened by the onset of the 1914–18 war. All branches of the industry were affected with the exception of two types of film-making—those of comedy and the detective serial—two branches in which the Paris studios had specialized. André Deed, French comedian of circus tradition and, further back, of the *Commedia del Arte*, created a character whom he called Gribouille, the simpleton hero with flour-daubed face, brother to Pierrot and Pagliaccio, and the personification of foolishness and gaucherie. A slightly more subtle type of humour was introduced by

11

Max Linder, schooled in vaudeville and tough down-town theatres, where this young actor from Bordeaux had served his apprenticeship. For his screen character 'Max', he chose a typical young man-about-town of the pre-1914 war. In private life he was of gay temperament, independent means, relieved by kindly fortune of the vulgar necessity of earning a living, free to devote himself entirely to the pleasures of life and love. Linder often wrote his own scripts and directed his films, steering clear of commonplace jokes and the by-now inevitable chases: he preferred to portray through his clowning a more subtle observation of humanity. His best films are in the short-story style, developing a deliberately slender dramatic theme with beauty and depth of expression. Linder was a long time learning his art, but he finally mastered it and became one of the greatest of comedians. Although his approach was direct and simple, he had mastered the art of suggesting a whole world of sentiment through the tiniest gesture; he had the secret of the light touch and perfect timing. His best films like *Max Victime du Quinquina* (Quinquina being a popular appetizer) and *Max Toréador*, are the true forerunners of the Chaplin masterpieces. The great British comedian has always been the first to acknowledge that Max Linder had been his teacher.

Max Linder's reputation quickly reached world-wide dimensions. Pathé signed him up with the promise of many hundreds of thousands of francs a year. And even before 1914 enthusiastic crowds everywhere from Berlin to Barcelona or St. Petersburg acclaimed him with thunderous applause. The cinema had revealed its first major, international star—indeed, the reign of stars was now to begin.

Linder soon had many imitators and rivals. The best known of these was the stage actor, Prince, known on the screen by the name of Rigadin; with his blank expression and turned-up nose, he was ideally suited to be the bewildered vaudeville buffoon. He sported striped trousers, frock-coat, bowler hat and fancy waistcoat—the costume of the French *petit bourgeois*. Unfortunately, his films, directed by Georges Monca and written by an assortment of mediocre writers, have not stood up to the test of time—we find them lacking in vigour, rhythm and sense of observation.

The same criticism might be made of the comedies made by Louis Feuillade for Gaumont Pictures, with the child actors Bébé and later Bout-de-Zan, as stars. Nevertheless, Feuillade had begun his film career in 1906 with a happy revival of the comic genre. With the systematic use of trick effects in open-air settings (according to the British example), he combined a sound, if somewhat pedestrian, sense of comic observation. He understood how, launching out with some absurd situation, it was possible to draw from it, with meticulous logic, a thousand lunatic consequences. In one of the best films he made at that time, *L'Homme Aimanté*, the hero buys himself a coat of mail as a protection against nocturnal attackers. Two young scamps magnetize the coat—whereupon coffee-pots, plates, iron tables, shop-signs, drain-covers, all attach themselves to the unhappy wearer. Escorted to the police-station, he is the cause of a burlesque dance of greeting performed by the swords of the police officers.

This same fantastical logic of the absurd appears again in the pictures of a pupil of Feuillade's, Jean Durand, director of two notable series, the *Onésime* and the *Calinoconis* (from the names of the central character). Durand was a more exacting artist than either Feuillade or even Max Linder, and in some of these films showed an exactness of editing which was later to become a lesson for the young René Clair. Durand also made a series of films *Dans Le Midi de La France* about wild animals and horse-back riders, partially inspired by the American Western, and starring Gaston Modet, Berthe Dagmar and Joe Hamman.

It fell to Louis Feuillade to be the most successful French director in another type of film—the serial detective story.

This kind of film was originated in 1908 by Victorin Jasset. Jasset, a former sculptor, had gained much experience by directing spectacular pageants or pantomimes, for which he designed the sets and costumes. Gaumont asked him to direct a film of the Passion. In this he showed a real gift for spectacular production, taking his inspiration directly from a series of water-colours painted by the Academician James Tissot, exhibited in the early years of the century. This *Vie de Notre Seigneur Jésus-Christ*, well-polished but rather conventionally stilted, was far less original than his *Nick Carter* series, adaptations from popular American novels then being published in France by a German firm. Jasset retained the names of the heroes, but moved the setting to Paris and there improvised adventures for his characters out of his own fertile imagination. The first *Nick Carter* series was a tremendous success and inspired other producers to promote other similar series of detective stories, like *Nat Pinkerton*; Jasset responded with adaptations of popular serial

13

stories appearing in the big daily papers—*Balaoo* by Gaston Leroux, and *Zigomar* by Léon Sazie. He then went on to direct yet another series called *Protéa*, which was cut short by his early death.

While Denola was directing *Rocambole*, a modern version of the famous popular novel by Ponson du Terrail, for Pathé, Louis Feuillade undertook for Gaumont his memorable series called Fantômas.

The central figure, a bandit in a black hood, had been created by two young popular novelists, Pierre Souvestre and Marcel Alain, who had published thirty-two volumes devoted to the fantastic exploits of their hero, *L'Empereur du Crime*. Successfully adapting to their own facile, fast-moving style of narration the method used by Zola in his *Rougon Macquart* cycle, the authors placed Fantômas, together with his mistress Lady Beltham, the detective Juve and the journalist Fander, in a succession of differing social environments.

Louis Feuillade wrote his scripts keeping closely with scrupulous care to the stories of these novels of Souvestre and Alain. Just as he had formerly transferred Méliès' most extravagant trick-shots into the open street, he staged the wild adventures of Fantômas against the real background of Paris and her suburbs; where interior studio reconstructions were indicated, his sets were furnished by the big Paris stores. And from this juxtaposition of meticulous realism on the one hand and impossible exploits on the other, there results a strange kind of poetry. In a deserted villa at Neuilly, a beautiful and noble woman wrings her hands in despair while a boa-constrictor, a frequent instrument of such modern crime, writhes its way along the pipes which convey the central heating. Juve and Fander, miraculously escaping from a blazing furnace of wine-barrels on a wharf at Bercy, come upon the scene just in time. But Fantômas, black-hooded and in black tights, submerges himself in the underground water-cistern, breathing through the neck of a broken bottle. The Master of Terror evades their clutches once again.

On screens throughout the world there flourished an abundance of masked bandits, complex and invincible criminals, vainly pursuing innocent and apparently invulnerable victims; Jasset and Feuillade had their imitators everywhere: in Italy, *Tigris* and *Za la Mort*, in Germany, *Homunculus*, in Denmark, *Le Docteur Gar el Hama*, in Austria, *Les Invisibles*, in Great Britain, *Lieutenant Daring* or *Ultus* and in the U.S.A., *The Perils of Pauline*, with Pearl White, directed for Pathé by the French director, Gasnier. The advent of war in 1914 made no break in

14

the growing French influence in this field. But the war hastened the collapse of the industry itself, through weakening the industrial sphere.

About 1910, France's supremacy in the world of cinema was perhaps more complete than the present supremacy of Hollywood. Approximately 60 to 70 per cent of imported films came from Paris studios, and those mainly from the three great firms of Pathé, Gaumont and Eclair.

In Great Britain, in 1909, according to Rachael Low, Pathé was exhibiting more films than all the British companies put together, and a similar situation existed in America. French firms had established important producing companies abroad—Gaumont-British in Britain, Pathé-Exchange in the U.S.A., Decla (Deutches Eclair) in Germany among the more notable. But soon the competition of the home industries of Italy, Denmark, Britain and, above all, America began to make itself felt on the International market; by 1914 the French stranglehold was already considerably weakened. The loss of grip was largely due to the persistence of French firms in clinging to old and circumscribed methods of production. They had hoped to retain their international monopoly by making low-budget pictures of a kind able to recover their costs in the home market alone, where exhibition was very greatly reduced.*

*There were 1,000 to 1,500 cinemas in France in 1914, as against some 5,500 in Great Britain.

III

THE FRENCH CINEMA
DURING THE WAR

1914—1919

2ND AUGUST 1914 turned the whole of Central Europe into a closed market for French films, and practically closed the important Russian market also. In the U.S.A., a vigorous home production, now perfectly attuned to the demand of its own public taste, rapidly eliminated the 'immoral' French films, which had always been a little too lax for Americans in their attitude to marital infidelity. Moreover, a now soaring rate of production in Hollywood secured a monopoly of 90 per cent of British programmes, as well as conquering many key markets in other parts of the world to which French films still had access. In Paris itself the serial *The Clutching Hand*, *The Cheat*, Thomas Ince's Westerns and the Mack Sennett and Charles Chaplin comedies were winning a dominant place in the cinemas for American productions. The leading French companies themselves accelerated the process by forcing their own films on the U.S. market, importing a large number of American productions for exhibition on their own circuits, and finally by cutting down considerably on their home production. The centre of world film-making deserted the banks of the Seine for the shores of the Pacific.

The mobilization of studio personnel and players had naturally interrupted production in a Paris threatened by German invasion. After 1915, Pathé and Gaumont resumed work. First of all they produced propaganda films like *Chantecoq* and *Coeur de Française*. But these did

16

not long enjoy public favour—they were extremely crude and over-simplified—and so there was a return to the style of the pre-war decade. Feuillade had great success with his serial films: *Les Vampires*, *Judex*, *La Nouvelle Mission de Judex*. Pathé produced a few films only, and these consisted of continuations of the interminable, insipid Rigadin comic series. Viewed as a whole—with one notable exception, the *Monte Christo* of Pouctal, a director who later made a somewhat free adaptation of Zola's *Travail*—the work of the war years was mediocre.

Nevertheless, the harsh period of hostilities saw the gradual formation of new ideas in the French cinema. In Paris, where all the theatres had long been closed for fear the frivolity of those at home should cause discontent in the trenches, the darkened cinema halls had become the refuge of a new public. Young men awaiting their mobilization papers, Louis Aragon, Philippe Soupault, Paul Eluard and André Breton, enthused over Musidora in black tights silhouetted in *Les Vampires*, or over the fair Pearl White. Following thc cxample of their elders, Max Jacob, Guillaume Apollinaire and Pablo Picasso, all devoted film lovers since well before 1914, they saw in the adventure film the purest expression of modern poetry. Philippe Soupault contributed 'cine-poems' to *avant-garde* reviews, and the first published work by Louis Aragon was a long and remarkable study on *Le Décor du Cinéma*. Patrons of the Ballets Russes, the disciples of Paul Claudel or Henri Bataille, now gathered at the Colisée (the first cinema to be opened on the Champs-Elysées) to enjoy the latest Thomas Ince or Chaplin. Louis Delluc, journalist, novelist and playwright, became the guide and theorist of the *avant-garde* audience by publishing in his popular *Paris-Midi* a series of articles which inaugurated the first column of independent film criticism. Until then, film 'critics' had been merely publicity agents, paid so much per line by the producers.

When starting this new venture, Louis Delluc declared his intention of bringing to the notice of his readers, the names of such directors who were, in his opinion, capable of founding a new French school of film-making to rival that of America, then at its peak of fame. The names he cited were: Georges Lacroix, André Antoine, Léon Poirier, Jacques de Baroncelli, Le Somptier, Mercanton, Hervil, Germaine Dulac and Abel Gance.

Shortly after directing a film *Les Ecrits Restent* in 1918, considered remarkable by Delluc, Georges Lacroix died suddenly. André Antoine,

17

founder of the Théâtre Libre, was at that time an ardent advocate of the film, a medium which gave him scope for the systematic use of natural settings on which he had many personal theories. But he made the mistake of working with scripts of definitely poor quality, although based on such famous masterpieces as *Les Frères Corses*, *Les Travailleurs de la Mer*, *La Terre*, *L'Arlésienne*. All these pictures, made outside the studios, have some fine pictorial effects, but are marred by the poor quality of their narrative which prevented them from ever being successful. It was not long before André Antoine abandoned the cinema to return to his first love, the theatre.

Léon Poirier and Jacques de Baroncelli—of whom we shall hear more later—have never risen, even in their best work, above the level of sound craftsmen, and they were still making films in 1950. Baroncelli, a former journalist, turned out films by the dozen during the war, mixing good and bad indiscriminately. Léon Poirier, a director of more sensitive disposition, was a nephew of the painter, Berthe Morizot, and had been the secretary of the Théâtre des Champs Elysées, built for the Ballets Russes. He made his cinema début before 1914 in commercial films. After demobilization, he returned to work on *Le Penseur* which failed from too subtle and intellectual a script; he then continued with a series of pictures based on the Arabian Nights stories, *Le Coffret de Jade*, *Les Trois Sultanes*, *Ames d'Orient*, and others. The last was a follow-up to a fashion created in France by the success of *La Sultane de L'Amour*, a Persian story produced with spectacular décor by Le Somptier and Burguet.

Mercanton and Hervil had served their apprenticeship in the Film d'Art movement. Mercanton, after making *La Reine Elisabeth*, had during the war directed a great propaganda film, with Sarah Bernhardt in the leading role, *Mères Françaises*. Later, under the influence of Antoine, the two men made films shot entirely outside the studio, many in Britain; in these they presented theories very close to those of the neo-realist Italian school of to-day. But, as in the case of Antoine's work, Mercanton and Hervil made the mistake of using poor script material. Their best film was undoubtedly *Miarka, la Fille à L'Ours*, which was adapted from a novel by Jean Richepin, in which the great actress, Réjane, made her last screen appearance. It was under Mercanton and Hervil that the young Marcel L'Herbier first worked for the cinema, writing scripts for their *Bouclette* and *Le Torrent*.

18

Madame Germaine Dulac, who started her film career in 1916 with *Soeurs Ennemies*, was a woman of great culture, who combined with a keen intelligence the quality of real sensibility. Unhappily, with many misgivings, she was obliged to give way to certain commercial necessities. Her war films such as *Venus*, *Victrix*, *Ames de Fous* and *Géo le Mystérieux* although suffering from the current vice of indifferent scripting, are none the less in some passages a full reflection of her passionate depth of feeling.

The forceful personality of Abel Gance dominated the French Cinema in the closing period of the war. During the difficult years of his youth he had joined the cinema as an actor and script-writer. With the energy of the self-taught he had been trying to raise money to enable himself to finish his studies, Heraclitus, Spinoza, Lao Tseu, Socrates, Confucius and Bergson, being his favourite authors. Although as early as 1912 he had directed the *Le Masque d'Horreur* with the great tragedian de Max, it was not until after 1914 that he made his real début as a director with *Un Drame au Château d'Acre*, *Le Fou de la Falaise*, *Ce Que les Flots Racontent*, *La Fleur des Ruines*, and a serial film *Barberousse*. After *Les Gaz Mortels*, *La Zone de la Mort*, *L'Héroïsme de Paddy*, he followed up and established himself with *Mater Dolorosa*, *La Dixième Symphonie*, and above all, with *J'Accuse*, a film that made a considerable impression.

In those films for which he himself had written the script, Gance showed that he has been considerably influenced by the American school, in particular by Thomas Ince and Cecil B. de Mille (D. W. Griffith was then virtually unknown on the Continent). His films break right away from the very clear-cut technique in narrative and cutting, the considered, sober treatment, the precise and judiciously-framed photography, the whole style of approach perfected in France by Feuillade. Gance was a romantic, with a soaring temperament, undamped by fear of ridicule. He launched forth into complex and grandiloquent plots, bringing artificial lighting into play as a means of expression, using and abusing half-lights and back lighting in the so-called Rembrandt style.

J'Accuse had been made in co-operation with the Army cinematograph service, but its war propaganda was misted over with a vague pacifism that aroused a cry of anti-militarism against the director. The war was then coming to an end, but amidst a sea of social troubles, and, like Ponctal and Georges Lacroix, Gance felt these troubles deeply. He

19

wanted, he wrote, to be at once the Victor Hugo and the Henri Barbusse of the Great War. His hero, mad since the Germans violated his wife and left her with child, is a poet of the trenches who claims that his name is *J'Accuse*. At his summons, when evening comes, the dead arise to fight with Vercingetorix at their head. Yet all these extravagances fail to overlay a power, a sincerity, and a sense of film, which, in his best work, puts Abel Gance in the same rank as Griffith. Among countrymen whose first demand has ever been for measure and proportion, he came as an untamed force from Nature, without logic or discipline, but of undeniable power.

When the bells of the Armistice had rocked to silence, and France returned to normal industrial production, far-seeing minds, among them that of Louis Delluc, could make some assessment of her film prospects, and their conclusions were not optimistic.

Many of the foremost French were working in other countries—(Léonce Perret, Albert Capellani, Maurice Tourneur in the U.S.A., Georges Lacroix and Henri Krauss in Italy, Mercanton, Denizot and René Plaisesty in Great Britain). Studios were old and out of date, their equipment less than second rate. Foreign competition was increasing. America, Germany, even Sweden outstripped the French in many directions. Audience figures were very much lower than in America, England or Germany, and there seemed little possibility of bettering this situation in a country where over half of the population was scattered about in communities of less than 1,500 inhabitants. Hardly a single foreign market could be found. The big firms declared they were about to cease production.

Charles Pathé set the example. He had stated to the French film world in general, in 1918, that the English-speaking markets were of vital importance and that the French film must cater for their taste, or go under. If the film-makers did not show immediately that they had grasped this necessity, Pathé would no longer maintain them. He would act as their publisher, in the book-world sense of the term, and contract to print and distribute a negative already completed, but he would decline to shoulder the financial risks of production.

When the directors did not respond to his ultimatum, Charles Pathé kept to his word. His company continued to provide big profits for its shareholders, by selling piece by piece, to the highest bidder, all its vast industrial and commercial equipment—the production plants in

America, England, Germany and Italy; whole exhibition circuits; studios; and, lastly, the new celluloid film factory at Vincennes. With a few isolated exceptions, Pathé left production and its attendant monetary risks to the little vassal producers in its distribution combine. This policy was dictated by the financial magnates who controlled the company. Declaring that, in their opinion, France, though victorious in the war, was now a second-class power without prospects for the future, they deliberately slowed down the industrial production of the country.

The French cinema was toppling from its eminence. And contrast with the real heights it had attained earlier made this breaking down the more tragic. But there was one man who dreamt of a revival. Louis Delluc, who unhappily understood only too clearly the extent of the decline, commented on it in print with an undisguised bitterness. But he dreamed, none the less, of the creation of a new French school. To this ideal he devoted, indeed sacrificed, his life, though he never saw its full realization.

IV

THE IMPRESSIONIST SCHOOL

1920—1927

THE group which gathered round Delluc—Germaine Dulac, Marcel L'Herbier, Abel Gance, and, a little later, Jean Epstein—was known as the Impressionist School. 'Impressionist' was a term Delluc himself often used in reference to the film; and it has the further advantage of throwing into relief the similarities, as equally the divergences, between the French films of this post-war period and their German contemporaries.

'The French cinema must be *cinema*: the French cinema must be *French*.' Such was the maxim Delluc printed large at the head of his review *Cinéma*, and he was the tireless exponent of his precept. 'Ah, that is good! That is *cinema*!' was his great expression of approval—an expression asserting the film as an art in its own right, having its own laws which must differentiate it from the other arts, and from literature and the theatre in particular. In reaction against the abuse of 'adaptation' since the introduction of that process in the Film d'Art, he demanded scenarios written solely and expressly for the screen, and set the example by writing his own.

While Delluc earnestly desired to see the French film *French*, an expression of national character, he was not at great pains to establish it in any line with the French cinema tradition as it had begun to evolve before the war. Until 1914, he himself abhorred the film, and had regarded the production of the pre-war years as of no value or interest. Of his French predecessors, he held in respect only Louis Lumière and Max Linder. Méliès was in all probability an unknown name to him. In Feuillade's work he acknowledged certain qualities, but on the whole his reaction to it was one of irritation—and justifiably so. After 1918, most of the pre-war directors had found themselves outdistanced by the rapid evolution of their own art, and they degenerated sadly, Feuillade among the first.

A national art, if it is to disown national tradition, must look for examples elsewhere. Passing over Italy—to the accompaniment of some scathing criticism (the film there was suffering a 'decline' also)—Delluc turned to America, to Thomas Ince and Chaplin more especially at first, and then, with the appearance of *Broken Blossoms*, to D. W. Griffith. (*Birth of a Nation* and *Intolerance* were not seen in France until after 1920, and so exerted little influence there.) He became a great admirer of the Swedish school, and helped his friend Moussinac to popularize its films in France after 1920, and also of the German expressionist movement; he was largely instrumental in introducing the latter to his countrymen, arranging the inaugural presentation in Paris of the famous *Cabinet of Doctor Caligari*.

But while he so strongly advocated the study of American, Swedish and German films, Delluc never supported the mere imitation of them. They were to provide but a school, and the lessons learnt were to be the basis, and only the basis, on which to build a new, distinctively national creation. His own first scenario, *La Fête Espagnole*, which was filmed by Mme Germaine Dulac, is a fair example of his creative method. The theme, set against an exotic background, is the rival passion of two men for one woman, and their savage battle to the death for her. This is a subject closely resembling creations of a scenario-writer for whom Delluc had a great admiration, Gardner Sullivan, then writing for Thomas Ince. But the French director sought his exotic setting in Spain instead of the far West, and portrayed characters who are in manner and temperament essentially Latin, many times removed from the American cowboys whose screen representative was at that time W. S. Hart.

In *Fièvre*, Louis Delluc's best film, he shows himself concerned less with plot than with the creation of 'atmosphere'. A Marseilles 'dive' is here the equivalent of a Thomas Ince 'saloon'. There is not one hero but fifty. The most important role in the drama is really played by the setting, and in Delluc's hands what is a poor enough bit of studio-rigged décor takes on a life of its own.

The photography, on a sober note throughout, makes considerable use of deep focus, so that in all the close-up shots one is constantly aware of the background of the Marseilles café. The film is 'impressionist' by its lightness and swiftness of touch, the *pointillisme* which it casts deftly here and there among these 'underworld' characters, singling out fleetingly one after another beautifully drawn 'type'. The film has also a great deal in common with contemporary German productions. The popularity of the subject, the attention paid to creation of atmosphere, the seeking after unity of time and place—in all these respects *Fièvre* bears a close resemblance to the films of the movement then making itself felt in Germany with Carl Mayer's *Scherben* and *Hintertreppe*. The explanation was a coincidence of artistic preoccupations; there was no question of mutual influence.

La Femme de Nulle Part shows perhaps the influence of the Swedish school, in the important part played in the film by landscape—in this case a beautiful, tree-shadowed town, standing like an oasis in the pebbly wastes along the banks of the Rhône that inspired Van Gogh. The theme of the film is one much favoured by playwrights of the period. A woman who in her youth broke away from the tethers of conventional middle-class society to adopt the life of adventure, comes back, long afterwards, to her former home, discovers that a return to the kind of life it embodies is impossible for her, and departs again. Here again Delluc worked within the convention of the three unities, with the part played in classical tragedy by the monologue here assigned to the 'flashback'. This latter device was one which Delluc had used (almost as systematically as Orson Welles in *Citizen Kane*) in one of his very early films, *Le Silence*, the soliloquy of an intending suicide.

Following in the steps of *Broken Blossoms*, and certain Swedish films, Delluc became increasingly interested in the presentation of the truly intimate psychological study. In this direction he received invaluable assistance from his wife, Eve Francis, who, coming from the theatre, where she had played in the works of Claudel, became the foremost actress of the impressionist group. There is a passage towards the end of *La Femme de Nulle Part* of unforgettable beauty, in which he shows her trudging in the fading evening light over the long, stony road. At such moments—and when he made his first film shot, of a child's ball rolling towards the spectator—Delluc reveals his true stature as both painter and poet.

But the director whose work most thoroughly typifies the ideas of the impressionist group—it was Delluc himself who applauded it most—is

Marcel L'Herbier. L'Herbier was a symbolist poet and a writer of plays 'à la Maeterlink', who first made contact with the cinema as a scenario-writer for Mercanton and Hergil. In those early days he had himself directed a little quasi-experimental film, *Phantasmes*, an important feature of which was the systematic use of a technique employed since 1900 in artistic still photography, but never hitherto introduced into film, that of the 'soft focus'. *Phantasmes*, however, was never exhibited, and L'Herbier first came before the public with *Rose France*, with a scenario written by himself, and *Le Bercail*, an adaptation of a play of Bernstein's. From the latter film he preferred to disassociate himself, declaring that it was made purely for commercial purposes. *Rose France*, a war film, financed by the French propaganda service, opened with a symbolic shot, a war-scarred hand clasping a rose. The audiences of the time found such a refinement somewhat bizarre.

L'Herbier crystallized the quality of his work with *L'Homme du Large* and the film that marked the peak of his achievement, *Eldorado*. *L'Homme du Large*, a very free adaptation of a Balzac novel, is the story of a fisherman's son 'gone to the bad', the despair of his father and his betrothed. In its use of the ever-present ocean and its granite shores, and in its skilful use of Breton folk-costume, this film bears the clear mark of Swedish influence.

Where Delluc had devoted his main energies to the scenario, those of L'Herbier were concentrated on beauty of photography. His lofty attitude towards the 'story' of a film is well reflected in his dismissal of the plot of *Eldorado* as 'a melodrama'. *Eldorado* depicts a Spanish 'dive'—a European 'saloon' like that of Marseilles in Delluc's *Fièvre*. Certain parts of the film—the Holy Week procession to Seville, for instance—are virtually documentary, and save for the interior setting of the 'Maison de Danses', all of it was shot in the sun-baked countryside of Spain, a procedure endowing many passages with vividly realistic effect.

But for L'Herbier, the content, subject matter, pictorial description even, was of infinitely less importance than the form. Typically an impressionist here, the vision of things he gives us tends always to be a subjective one. His hero, a young Swedish painter (played by Jacques Catelain) studies a 'motif' —and the audience finds itself suddenly seeing this motif as the painter himself sees it—in a hazy, distorted vision, as might have been taken by a belated disciple of Monet. L'Herbier gives us the world through the eyes of the painter; elsewhere, he has given it us through the eyes of a drunkard; elsewhere again, and this in some of his best passages, using all the combined resources of photography (pictorial composition, soft focus) he gives it through the eyes of the director—the wall that towers with the inevitability of fate over the tragic despair of Eve Francis, or the dramatic dancing shadows on the backcloth behind the stabbed and dying ballerina.

The wall recalls a famous scene from *Dr. Caligari*, the shadows a passage from Robison's *Scherben*. But here again one must be careful not to interpret as interchange of influences between French impressionism and German expressionism what was, in fact, but a striking coincidence in their artistic preoccupations. L'Herbier had not yet seen *Dr. Caligari*, nor Robison *Eldorado*.

When he did meet the work of the German expressionist school (through the intermediary offices of Delluc), the experience came to L'Herbier as a profound shock, and threw him seriously out of his artistic stride. He embarked upon a *Don Juan et Faust*, a very ambitious piece of work, which reached a degree of obscurity it had hardly the profundity to justify. Some shots were composed on the model of cubist pictures, with the actors, their faces made up in a motley of colours, stuck into painted cardboard boxes. The vogue for 'Caligarism' threatened to turn the cinema into a kind of magic lantern show of a series of modern paintings.

In spite of its ingenious shots, and the strangeness of the costumes designed for it by the young Claude Autant-Lara, *Don Juan et Faust* was a failure. 'Caligarism' had exaggerated L'Herbier's weaknesses, without in compensation endowing his work with any intensity, or even warmth. Coldness continued to be the most conspicuous defect of an over-refined aesthete.

L'Inhumaine was another ambitious film. The scenario was the work of Pierre MacOrlan, then enjoying a reputation made with the success of *Cavalière Elsa* (in which a fair 'revolutionary' conquers Paris at the head of an 'Asiatic horde'.) *L'Inhumaine*, played by Georgette Leblanc, former muse of Maeterlinck, was a kind of super-vamp, with a whole retinue of admirers—a Hindu prince, a mysterious political agitator, and a young industrialist. The lush and grotesque scenario was in the tradition of the older Danish and Italian films. Despite the services of a whole galaxy of contemporary talent—the modern architect Mallet Stevens, the young designer Alberto Cavalcanti, the composer Darius

26

Milhaud, the artist painter Fernand Léger—the film was almost a total failure, with profession and public alike. In many respects, its errors and extravagances marked the end of the impressionist movement.

Abel Gance was a man of strong individuality who could never have brought himself to be more than 'on the margin' of any school. Alongside the cold distinction of Marcel L'Herbier, his film *La Roue* came as something of tremendous verve, bubbling over, with much style but not a great deal of taste—a volcano emitting flame indeed, but also its quota of lava and slag. To the making of this film (in which the influence of Griffith is very marked) there went three years of work, superhuman toil, and enormous capital expenditure. An over-extravagant scenario was written in an attempt to achieve the timeless, universal significance of the epic. The hero, an engine driver, was intended as the modern reincarnation of Oedipus and Sisyphus. Euripides, Zola, Victor Hugo and the worst of the penny novelettes were all mixed up together to produce a final result of wildly extravagant episodes (totalling some 10,000 of 15,000 feet of film) united by a common mood of extreme, and often exasperating, romanticism.

The film was made almost entirely outside the studio: in dispensing after this fashion with interior resources, Gance was following the theories of Antoine and Mercanton. Shooting was done in the Alps, and on the shunting tracks of Nice railway station. Where sets were necessary, they were built 'on location'—the hero's house, for instance, all adorned with artificial flowers, was set up there and then between the tracks. A few scenes only were shot in studio sets.

The true hero of *La Roue*, quite ousting from that position the improbable character of the engine driver, is the railway. The key to the film is *La Chanson du Rail*, a piece which was later to be the inspiration for Arthur Honegger's famous *Pacific 231*. *Intolerance* had awakened Gance to the effectiveness of speedier cutting; a marked trend in contemporary painting had developed in him a sense of the plastic values inherent in moving machinery. The fortunate combination resulted in several really beautiful passages of film. Such passages, together with the power, the sincerity, and the personality that come through so strongly in this film, finally take precedence over and outweigh all the lapses into the puerile, the sentimentally naïve, or the merely extravagant. Certain parts of the 'cinematographic cathedral' Gance was endeavouring to raise have not stood the test of time, but

27

the surviving ruins are of an impressive grandeur; and there are a few passages worthy of inclusion in the most selective anthology, where the director comes very near to the realization of his great ambition to be the Victor Hugo of the cinema.

While Gance was putting the finishing touches to his *La Roue*, fresh blood was finding its way into the impressionist movement. The newcomer was the young Jean Epstein. Theorist, amateur philosopher, and a bold and scintillating essayist, Epstein had just given proof of an interest in film with a series of publications, poems and manifestos in which he sang the praises of Chaplin, Nazimova, Fairbanks, Charles Ray, W. S. Hart, and others of the Hollywood studios. Louis Delluc and Léon Moussinac signified their approval of these essays and encouraged the writer. Finally Epstein tried his own hand at film-making, working with Jean Benoit-Lévy on an official documentary about the work of Pasteur, parts of which were of great beauty. There followed *L'Auberge Rouge*, an adaptation from Balzac, and then *Le Coeur Fidèle*, a film which was immediately and deservedly acclaimed, and which none of his later work was to surpass.

The theme of *Le Coeur Fidèle* was one which had earlier formed the basis of *La Fête Espagnole*—the rivalry of two men in love. The film was admired in particular for its *morceau de bravoure*, a fairground scene—with roundabouts, shots taken from moving swingboats, bumper cars, crowds, close-ups of faces, all put together in a passage of 'accelerated cutting'. Like the *Chanson du Rail*—though without its authenticity and power—this fairground passage represents the code of aesthetics fashionable in 1923.

But what chiefly strikes us to-day about *Cœur Fidèle* is the 'popular' nature of its subject and setting. This *populisme* was in fact, and paradoxically enough, one of the major contributions to the cinema of this whole group of directors, over and above their characteristic impressionist technique. The note is struck in all the key films of the movement—*Fièvre, Eldorado, L'Homme du Large, La Roue*. At a time when Hollywood was turning increasingly to the luxurious studio set, and peopling it increasingly with millionaires and *femmes fatales*, the French cinema, following in the tradition of the early films of Ince and Griffith, retained its fondness for the open air, and included in its scope—to a limited degree—the expression of social realities. To be sure, it betrayed more interest in the life of the underworld than in that of the working classes. But its directors were alive to the pictorial possibilities of the big sea-port or the fairground, the bistro or the dive. True heirs to the tradition of the great French novelists and the impressionist painters, they endowed these scenes instinctively with poetry, significance, plastic value. Moreover, some such normality of setting was to them an artistic necessity; let them attempt to dispense with it, to cast loose from the anchoring structure of reality, and their films lose balance, direction, gripping power. *L'Inhumaine* forfeits interest through the absurdly abstracted intellectualism of its construction; while *Le Coeur Fidéle* still stirs our sympathies to-day by its very fidelity to everyday life.

By the end of the twentieth century, our children will doubtless be telling us that they find it hard to distinguish between certain passages of Delluc and Feuillade, Gance and Jasset, Epstein and Zecca. These men share a certain common quality of sensitivity, peculiarly French, and a common visualization of the everyday life of the people.

After *Coeur Fidéle*, Epstein directed *La Belle Niéernaise*, centring round the life of the watermen whose barges travel the French canals—a theme taken up later by Vigo.

The work of Germaine Dulac reflects all the qualities of this remarkable woman—intelligence, refinement, sensitivity. Unfortunately, it is too often based on grandiloquent, improbable stories. *La Mort du Soleil*, for instance, is completely spoilt by the incongruous relation of character and plot. We are introduced to a scientist of genius, whose work overshadows that of a Pasteur or a Mme Curie, but whose life is apparently a sequence of trivial, childish adventures. The many passages of real beauty fail to-day to redeem the basic mediocrity of the plot, the unreal nature of which may have been a concession on Mme Dulac's part to the real or supposed taste of her public.

Her best films are those in which she had the initial services of a good scenario-writer—Louis Delluc for *La Fête Espagnole*, André Obey for *La Souriante Madame Beudet*. Of the former work there has come down to us only the scenario, also an extract too brief to form a basis for any assessment of the whole. But the second, which we have intact, is of real significance. It is an adaptation from a theatrical play in which the author illustrates the theory that silence is often more eloquent

29

than words. The film depicts the household of a provincial businessman with a wife, a second Mme Bovary, a devotee of the muses, and so repulsed by the excessive coarseness of her husband that she attempts to kill him. But this 'accident' is prevented, and the couple sink back into their drab rut of provincial monotony.

This middle-class tragedy, involving only two characters, has the same tone with the same slender tautness of theme as a Maupassant stort story. The psychological analysis is truer to life, and the characters more thoughtfully developed, than was usually the case in the days of silent film. There is a close resemblance to be traced between this portrayal in half-tones and an exactly contemporary German film, *Sylvester*. But the *intimisme* of Mme Dulac and the *Kammerspiel* of Lupu Pick and Carl Mayer are not the fault of reciprocal influence The obsession of the German film with an oppressive fate, its frenzied passions, its Teutonic extravagances—none of these has any counterpart in the work of the French director. The husband's characteristics are brought out, a little clumsily perhaps, but without deliberate exaggeration. And a few details in the direction—as a vase moved first by one, then by the other of the couple—are there for a definite purpose within the story such as the revelation of character and the creation of atmosphere; they are not intended to have any meaning outside the framework of this particular film, and no pretension is made to endow them with the kind of symbolic significance, heavy with metaphysical mystery, so beloved by the German directors.

The year 1924 saw the death of Louis Delluc at the age of thirty-two —exhausted by the struggle he had waged for the creation of a French school in the cinema. His last film was a minor one, *L'Inondation*, completed just before he died. The impressionist movement did not long survive him. Mme Dulac was soon to leave its ranks to deploy her talents in the field of the *avant-garde*, and, after a number of failures, Jean Epstein became a fabricator of vaguely expressionist films for a few specialized exhibitors—*Six et Demi, Onze*; *La Chute de la Maison Usher*; *La Glace a Trois Faces*. It was left to L'Herbier and Gance to carry the faults of the movement to the extremes dictated by their respective temperaments, and, in so doing, complete its liquidation.

Abel Gance, whose unbounded energy could conjure funds as it seemed out of the air, began work in 1923 on *Napoléon*. He took four years to complete it. Film was used up in hundreds of millions of feet.

30

He mobilized the cream of the profession in actors, technicians, directors, designers, and galvanized them into feverish activity with speeches coined from the best Bonapartian tradition. But in spite of the years spent in production, and the reels of film covered, Gance got no further with the biography of his hero than the crossing of the Alps for the first Italian campaign. The narration confines itself to Napoleon's schooldays at the Collège de Brienne, a scene of life in Corsica, a few days during the Revolution, and the siege of Toulon. But an eagle perched constantly on the young officer's shoulder, and the words 'Saint-Helena' occurring continually in the schoolboy's exercise book, appear as prophetic reminders of the hero's future destiny.

Historically and psychologically, the film was third-rate or worse, and it unconsciously caricatured both Napoleon (of whom Gance was a great admirer) and the Revolution (which he abhorred). But again we find these deficiencies carried off by the sheer ebullient temperament of the director. Bonaparte hunted through Corsica by the Seides of Paoli, in a wild horse chase directly inspired by the 'Western', then escaping in a boat with a tricolor as a sail; Danton teaching the 'Marseillaise' to a wildly enthusiastic Convention with Rude's bas-relief of the march of the army of Year II through the St. Bernard Pass into Italy coming through in a superimposure—these are passages of almost epic force, the work of a master.

Speeded cutting had been the great innovation of *La Roue*. In *Napoléon*, this technique was relegated to the background, but Gance made great use of the 'triple screen' and the 'subjective camera'.

The triple-screen procedure consisted simply in the placing of two screens of equal size, one on either side of the central one. The audience was thus presented with a very wide field of vision, and projection by this method, although only a few cinemas could adopt it, made a great impression.

The 'subjective camera' technique was a further development of the systematic use of the 'travelling shot' recently introduced by Murnau in his *The Last Man*. The frequent employment of this technique had been made possible by the manufacture in France of light, portable cameras, in which the old for-ever-turning handle was replaced by a clockwork mechanism or a compressed air motor. In *Eldorado*, L'Herbier had given a view of the world as seen through the eyes of one of his characters; but it had had perforce to be the world seen from a

31

virtually static point of view, the point of view of the contemplating painter. In *Napoléon*, using the portable camera, Gance brings to the screen the world as it appears to the characters engaged in excited action and violent physical movement. In the Corsican man-hunt, a camera was lashed to one of the galloping horses, to shoot the surrounding countryside as it would have been seen by Bonaparte in his flight. Then the apparatus was encased in a waterproof box and hurled from the top of the cliffs into the Mediterranean, to record exactly the visual impressions of Bonaparte as he dived. When it came to the siege of Toulon, a miniature camera was enclosed in a football, which was then tossed violently into the air—the world through the eyes of a soldier hurled upwards by a cannon ball!

When the portable camera was put into the hands of L'Herbier, he was drunk with the new joyful possibilities into which he plunged wholesale. With the lack of discrimination that belongs only to the intoxicated, he made a film adapted from a novel by *L'Argent*. This follows in the chronology of L'Herbier's work a good film based on Pirandello's novel *Feu Mathias Pascal* and a bad one devised from Lucie Delarue-Mardrus's novel *Diable au Cœur*.

L'Argent, a lavish Franco-German production, transposed Zola's novel into the France of its own day—a procedure which brought down on L'Herbier's head some vehement reproaches from André Antoine. The ruling spirit of the Théâtre Libre claimed that Zola's novel was inseparable from the setting of the Bourse, as it had been in the period 1860-80, in the days of Manet, Auguste Renoir and Degas.

In actual fact, the novel served L'Herbier as little more than a pretext. In his hands, the financial intrigues that were the main theme of the book were relegated to the background, and an originally minor character, Baroness Sandorf, became the central figure—this largely in order to furnish a role for Brigitte Helm. Like *L'Inhumaine*, *L'Argent* is a film of amorous intrigue in lavish modern interiors, and here the 'portables' are let loose in a veritable ballet of their own—withdrawing, advancing, dropping from ceilings and rising from the floor, turning in circles like horses on a roundabout. The Bourse, virtually the hero of Zola's book, dwindles to nothing more than a picturesque décor. Subjective impressionism, sacrificing everything to the search after new developments of vision and originality of camera angle, had come finally to a complete negation of man and society—to treating them

32

simply as forms, shadows, visual objects, to be patterned in an abstract geometry.

This contemptuous disregard of the claims of content that characterized the impressionist movement in its decadence, together with the attitude of general disdain it affected towards the public, led to failures —all the more disastrous as expenditure on production had usually been heavy. It would be doing an injustice, however, to attribute the failures entirely to the excesses of temperament, preferences for the ivory tower or intransigent individualism. Both L'Herbier and Epstein, for instance, accepted the necessity of making commercial films on a level of subject matter they held in contempt, justifying the time spent on such unrewarding material by using it as a field for technical, formal research. And, increasingly, the conditions of French film production were making it more difficult to undertake other enterprises. Since 1920, the French cinema industry had been sliding ever more rapidly into a slump; the export of films to other countries had practically ceased— and the advances of the Impressionist group from 1923 onwards, systematically discouraged by the big combines, remained unknown abroad and excited virtually no influence. If the movement disintegrated so soon, it was largely because forces over which it had no control confined it in a closed circle.

In 1929, French film production, fifteen years earlier the most considerable in the world, had fallen to fifty full-length films a year—and all were mediocre. Even in France, the standing of the French film had been lost—an American film, a German, or a Russian took easy precedence, at all levels of society. The big firms, in face of an even more difficult financial situation, were refurbishing old subjects already worn threadbare, placing even more reliance on 'star' attraction than on sound direction, and busy attempting to negotiate international combines (these with Germany in particular). The formalism and cosmopolitanism which were to destroy the impressionist movement were due, in great measure, to the pressure of economic and social circumstances.

Moreover, the work of Delluc and his associates was not without valuable fruit. This group of men was the first in Europe to assert the stature of the film as an art—the equal (or even the superior) of music, literature, and the theatre—and to obtain recognition for it as such. With the creation of independent film criticism they gave body and

33

substance to their claim. Following the appearance in the famous literary journal *Mercure de France* of a series of articles on the cinema by perhaps the most outstanding of this first generation of critics, Léon Moussinac, nearly every published paper, from the major reviews to the dailies and weeklies, made way besides its section of drama criticism for a section devoted to film. Henceforward, the cinema became a subject of dinner-table conversation like the novel or the play, and there emerged a group among the intellectual *élite* for whom it was a major artistic preoccupation.

With the idea of fostering the growth of this new public, Delluc had founded his Ciné Club—intending that it should develop into a vast organization of film spectators, on a similar scale to the famous Touring Club. This latter goal he did not attain, but, with Canudo and Moussinac, he did organize the first film exhibitions that commanded the same kind of interest as a concert or an exhibition of paintings. And, from the seeds here sown, there sprang up the Ciné-Club, or Film Society movement, that was to flourish first in Paris and then with sturdy, rapid increase in the provincial cities. One of the off-shoots of the movement, through a Ciné-Club that turned commercial enterprise, was the creation of the specialist cinemas (Le Vieux Colombier, Studio des Ursulines, le Studio 28), where a faithful and enthusiastic public could see films which were out of the ordinary. It was the existence of these cinemas and of the Ciné-Clubs that enabled the young *avant-garde* movement to find itself an audience.

V

THE AVANT-GARDE

1923—1933

THE movement which we have referred to as 'impressionist' has sometimes also been termed *la première avant-garde*. But Delluc and his associates, students of the schools of symbolism, the Ballets Russes, the theories of Gordon Craig, and the more advanced trends in academic painting, had little in common with the artistic and literary *avant-garde*, stemming from Cubism and the Futurist movements, which in the early 1920's was evolving along the paths of Dadaism and Surrealism.

Since 1918, in the little Dadaist reviews published in Paris and Zürich, theorists had been postulating the film without a subject. In 1923 this theory was for the first time carried out by an American photographer working in France, Man Ray, in a film he ironically called *Le Retour à la Raison*. The film was first exhibited during the big manifesto assembly known as the Cœur à Barbe, and remembered as the occasion of violent dissensions, from which the Dadaist movement emerged split in two rival factions. It was a short work, distinguished by the fleetingness and indeterminacy of its images—leaving the spectator with the impression of having been looking through a kaleidoscope. The only pictures to be discerned at all clearly were those of the interior mechanism of a watch, labelled 'Danger', and the upside-down torso of a naked woman, seen through moving zebra-effect strips of light and shade. There was no strong rhythm to unite the film; the dominating factor appeared to be a striving after shock-effect and sensation. It resembled very much a collection of animated versions of the abstract still-photographs Ray was publishing in the Dadaist reviews—though it must not be imagined as in any way stylistically akin to the films of animated designs, moving geometric figures, then being produced in Germany by Hans Richter and Walter Ruttmann after the example of the Dadaist Vikking Eggeling.

Then came the *Ballet Mécanique* of Fernand Léger and Dudley Murphy, variations executed with the plastic objects so beloved of the cubist painter—metal balls, bits of machinery, limbs of models, oddments from the bazaar, bits of fairground equipment, posters, newspaper headlines. These were animated, and their movements combined in what was indeed a mechanical ballet—in which, from time to time, were also shots of washer-women climbing a staircase.

But the most famous Dadaist film was *Entr'acte* directed by René Clair, and based on a scenario by Francis Picabia. The latter curious character, essayist, painter, and poet, enjoyed in his time a reputation equal to Picasso's to-day. It was he among the Dadaist group who carried to the furthest their characteristic love of the extravagant and of the gratuitous manifestation. In 1925, he had been commissioned by Rolf de Maré, of the Ballets Suédois, to compose a ballet. The work completed, Picabia called it *Relâche* with the intention of misleading into his auditorium the snobs hastening to a genuine Champs-Elysées intermission. *Entr'acte* was the film version of *Relâche*.

With this film, René Clair came for the first time as a director before the public. A young Parisian, son of a wealthy businessman, he dreamed of becoming a novelist, but had taken a job on a newspaper while seeking a publisher. Resigned to the need of a surer living, he turned film-actor, played in films of Loie Fuller (*Le Lys de la Vie*), of Protozanav (*Le Sens de la Mort*) and of Feuillade (*Les Deux Gamines Parisette*). But his real ambition still lay elsewhere, as shown by his adoption of a pseudonym for work in the cinema; his real name, Chomette, was reserved for the literary title-page.

It is probable that Clair shared the enthusiasm of his Dadaist contemporaries for *Fantômas* and *Les Vampires*. Certain it is that he never despised the films of the pre-war period, the comics *à la* Jean Durand, and he held it no disgrace to play in serial films—ciné-novels, as they were called at the time. Indeed, he was bold enough to prophesy that these latter would find greater favour with posterity than the film of artistic pretensions. He proclaimed himself a disciple also of Chaplin and Mack Sennett.

Entr'acte was a synthesis of the traditions of *l'avant-guerre* (gleaned by Clair from Feuillade) with the notions of the *avant-garde* as represented by Picabia and the Dadaists. The film runs deliberately to incoherency and with a desire to shock—'it respects nothing, save possibly the need for sudden bursts of laughter'. To read a constructive theme on traditional lines into it would be to mistake its purpose altogether. Clair and Picabia worked within a conception akin to the Dadaist conception of poetry, with a primary search after the bizarre surprise effect. The skirt of a ballet dancer opens and closes in slow motion, like flower-petals in the scientific film where the motion of nature is accelerated. The dancer jostles for a place on the screen with chimneys, rooftops, jets of water. Gradually the face of the dancer is revealed—it has a thick black beard and steel-rimmed pince-nez. Dadaist use of explosive metaphor, surprise-effect, mystification. There is throughout *Entr'acte* an underlying mockery of *les snobs*, to whom the film was presented on a gigantic screen as if towering over their puny beings, while the orchestra played a rhythmic irony by Eric Satie.

Satie played a part in the film, as did also the Dadaists Marcel Duchamp and Man Ray, and Jean Borlin, leading dancer of the Ballets Suédois. The latter is seen being shot down by Picabia in a fairground shooting range with a gun the shape of a clay pipe. A number of solemn-faced gentlemen, in top hats and black suits, come slowly gambolling behind a hearse drawn by a camel, and then in a suburb of Paris we see a mad pursuit party setting out. Clair brought into play all the arts of superimposition, quick cutting and trick photographic effects made fashionable by the Impressionist movement—but using them as a medium which was not allowed to obtrude and distract attention from the central action of the film. This was evidenced by the pursuit of the hearse by classic characters of the old films—until finally, the corpse returns to life and whisks everyone away, himself included.

The editing of *Entr'acte* was carried out with meticulous regard for detail and a minute, watch-maker-like precision. This precision, and the preference for a delicate, slender, central theme, are characteristic of René Clair throughout his career. *Paris Qui Dort* his first film, but which he edited only after *Entr'acte*, was based on a similar simplicity: what would happen if a scientist, by means of some secret ray, were to immobilize Paris? The idea might well have furnished an episode for Feuillade's *Vampires*. But Clair treats it differently. The ironical humour

37

of the former is always, as it were, in abeyance; in the work of his pupil, on the other hand, humour suffuses everything. And the younger director consciously develops one of the instinctive endowments of Feuillade, his feeling for the poetry of Paris. The Eiffel Tower is the central personnage of *Paris Qui Dort*—a film made with equipment barely superior to that of an amateur.

The great dispute of Cœur à Barbe had split Dadaism into two groups. While the 'orthodox' faction, partisans of Picabia and Tristan Tzara dispersed, the dissenters led by Breton, Aragon, Paul Eluard proclaimed the death of Dadaism and the birth of the new movement they called Surrealism. In the cinema, Dadaism achieved expression in *Entr'acte* then faded out. The movement had a more lasting development in Germany, where under the influence of theorists like Van Daesbourg, de Moholly Nagy, and Mondrian, it became that of the 'Abstract Film', or 'Pure Cinema'. The abstract trend never took any real root in France. It had one strenuous advocate there in the person of the Comte de Beaumont, the Maecenas who launched the Soirées à Paris in would-be rivalry to the Ballets Suédois. The film he financed, *Reflets de Lumière et de Vitesse*, with the alternative title *A Quoi Rêvent les Jeunes Films* was directed by the younger and less gifted brother of René Clair, Henri Chomette. Its sequence of views of dead branches, projected from the negative, and interspersed with images of crystal knife-rests, contrived to be more wearisome than abstract, and exerted little influence.

Surrealism made its aggressive cinema début at the Studio des Ursulines, with *La Coquille et le Clergyman*, made by Germaine Dulac and based on a scenario by Antonin Artaud. Artaud, a poet of the symbolist movement, was also an actor; among other parts he had played that of Marat in the *Napoléon* of Abel Gance. He had expected to play the principal role in *La Coquille et le Clergyman*, and though in fact it was given to someone else, simply because he (Artaud) had been ill, he was convinced that there had been treachery afoot, and created a disturbance at the première with a rowdy Surrealist demonstration.

The film was not altogether successful. Germaine Dulac's directness of approach and the complex subtleties of Artaud made uncomfortable bedfellows. The subject, encumbered with many psychoanalytic trappings, is the dream-world of a repressed and impotent priest in which he pursues his ideal woman, and struggles against a rival who is by turn fellow-priest, general, and prison-gaoler. The hero is seen smashing

38

hundreds of glass balls in an underground cellar, or crawling on all fours in an ankle-length overcoat through the streets of Paris. The final impression is one of moroseness rather than of humour. There is little force felt to-day in this first Surrealist essay. Another Surrealist picture, on the other hand, *Le Chien Andalou*, has lost nothing of its startling virulence.

The scenario of *Le Chien Andalou* is the work of Luis Bunuel and Salvador Dali. It is as devoid as *Entr'acte* of any thread of logical coherence. The world of the film is one of poetry, its object the expression in direct visual metaphor, of feelings and the vibrations of the soul. In the choice of metaphorical symbol there is the same tendency as in *Entr'acte* for what will startle or shock. The eye of a young woman slashed in two with a razor, two grand pianos each draped with the rotting carcase of a donkey, a hermaphrodite in a Paris street standing staring at a mutilated hand, the hero shot down by his double, an ants' nest in the palm of a clenched fist—such were the violent attractions of a tragic, brutal film. It was directed by Bunuel in a bare, impersonal style recalling the earlier work of Feuillade—and which, in its objectivity, heightened the shattering violence of the work. For the rest, the dominant influence of the Surrealist movement was clear, and precluded the attempt to find a rational core to the film or a central theme of psychoanalytic speculation.

Deliberate, planned absurdity had been the motive force in arranging the sequence of the scenes, the arbitrary juxtaposition of incongruous objects—but *Le Chien Andalou* is none the less symbolic of the state of mind of a generation. *Entr'acte* had been a mad but joyous throwing-over of the traces, of carefree students in an as yet unthreatened world. After 1925, however, the young intellectuals found themselves harassed by the social problems of their time. Especially was this true of those who, like our script-writers, had been born into the feudal backwardness and simmering discontent of pre-Revolutionary Spain. In Bunuel's own words, *Le Chien Andalou* was 'a despairing passionate call to the slaughter'. Like André Breton, the script-writers claimed that 'the simplest Surrealist action of all would be to go down into the street and shoot at random into the crowd'. Beneath this anarchistic state of mind, there could be felt, spasmodic, violent, ambivalent, the revolt of young intellectuals against the world which had brought them forth, and from which they had not yet disengaged themselves.

Le Chien Andalou cannot be said to have created a school. The gloomy *Sang d'un Poète* made not long afterwards by Jean Cocteau, was in some respects an imitation of it—the hero holds in his palm a speaking mouth which invites comparison with Bunuel's ant-heap. But the film occupied very much the same position as a new coat-of-arms—made up of symbols, easily deciphered by the spectator having the slightest acquaintance with the heraldic symbol system. Hotel rooms filled with the oppressive breath of opium, plastercast women barely fair enough for their purpose (driving incredibly beautiful young men to suicide), bare-torso poets, crowned and robed in the manner of antiquity, secret hermaphrodite amours, angelic negresses in inviting half-dress. All this autobiographical bric-à-brac, carried to the last pitch of refinement, gave off as it were an odour of decomposition. Its moments of sincerity, nearly always involuntary, were confined to the representation of manners. Cocteau's film, supreme expression of decadence, was the pillar of salt left beside the ruins of the Surrealist *avant-garde*.

In *L'Age d'Or*, Bunuel's second film, dating like *Sang d'un Poète* from the first days of the sound-track, the director returns to skilful manipulation of symbols and allegory. 'My love, my love, my love'—repeats the voice of Paul Eluard, while the lovers, eyes crushed out and hands gnawed away, roll on the gravel of an alleyway. A quasi-mystical conception of love, as transfigurer, almost redemptor, runs through a work that for the rest hurls itself in blasphemous assault against charity, religion, modesty, convention, the established order, and would trample them all in the dust. Angry scorpions, lava from erupting Vesuvius and other documentary passages alternate with scenes of most artificial contrivance—a cow lying in the bed of a young girl, Christ transformed into the Marquis de Sade, a giraffe and a flaming pine-tree thrown from a balcony, a blind man being trampled underfoot, a son being shot down by his father. Elsewhere, these pictorial metaphors have a most direct significance—the big reception, for instance, where the guests have their faces covered with flies, and behave as if unaware of the fires and explosions killing the serving-maids, and the huge tumbril that lumbers across the salon. Through the Surrealist extravagance and anarchic *scandale* comes the thin end of the wedge of social criticism.

Man Ray, like Bunuel, was a Surrealist, but his films differ markedly from *L'Age d'Or* or *Le Chien Andalou*. In the work of this director, for whom the brush was as congenial a means of expression as the camera,

40

plastic values take easy precedence over matters of scenario. He has an interest in the contrivance of photographic effects that at times brings his work very close to the L'Herbier impressionism—the excessive use of soft focus that blurs our vision of the characters in *Étoile de Mer*, for instance, recalls immediately our viewing of the Alhambra through L'Herbier's camera in *Eldorado*. Elsewhere, he devotes himself to piling up on his screen geometrical objects, of chess-board combinations (*Emak Bakia*), combining, like another Surrealist, Marcel Duchamp, meticulously calculated revolutions of geometrical curves with the strange puns of Rose Selavy. The scenarios of *Étoile de Mer* and *Emak Bakia* were the work of the poet Robert Desnos. But the films that issued from the studios of Duchamp and Man Ray had a cool precision, distinguished, intelligent, which obtained for them readier acceptance with a public Bunuel's ardent sincerity had only shocked.

Dadaism and Surrealism were the chief paths along which the *avant-garde* movement developed. But there were several young directors 'on the margin' of the school, producing films more or less in conformity with its ideas, but distinguished by the mark of an individual artistic personality, Jean Grémillon, for instance. Grémillon had begun his career making documentaries, with Périnal as his chief photographer, but a bare minimum of equipment. From a selection of the best passages of these documentaries, by means of skilful editing, he subsequently produced *Le Photogénie Mécanique*. Later, again with Périnal, he went to Brittany to make *Tour au Large*, a highly stylized picture of this coastal region and the sea, a succession of lovely images worked into a symphony.

Another of these marginal *avant-garde* directors was Alberto Cavalcanti, who had first entered the cinema world as a scenic designer (it was he who designed the very remarkable sets for L'Herbier's *Feu Mathias Pascal*, anticipating Orson Welles in the great use he made of ceilings). His first essay in direction, *Rien que des Heures*, was a dawn-to-dusk chronicle of the streets of Paris—a theme of sure public appeal. Then came *La P'tite Lilie* a burlesque adaptation of a popular song, with which Cavalcanti, his thoughts on similar pre-war successes, hoped to achieve in France what Mack Sennett had done in America, and inaugurate a French comic renaissance. The cast of *La P'tite Lilie* was made up of Jean Renoir and his wife, the actress Catherine Hessling, and certain of their friends. The same distinguished company played again in a later Cavalcanti film *Le Petit Chaperon Rouge*. Jean Renoir on his own account, after that most sensitive film *La Fille de l'Eau*, tried his hand at burlesque with *Charleston*. But neither Renoir nor Cavalcanti had the true comic gift. Their film in this genre never really achieved greater significance than that of a private joke.

René Clair was not very much more successful on his excursion into the realm of fantasy. His *Voyage Imaginaire*, intended as a kind of tribute to Méliès, who was then being rediscovered, fails for lack of rhythm and invention. Renoir, however, came to happier terms with fantasy, striking a note of real poetry with *La Petite Marchande d'Allumettes*. He brought to this adaptation of Hans Andersen's famous tale a wealth of technical contrivance, and succeeded in creating a true fantasy-world ballet.

But fantasy, comic or poetic, could not rescue the French *avant-garde* from the slough of despond of the 'twenties and their economic decline. Abstraction created at most a cool response from the French public. The obscure André Sevry, patiently filming the revolutions of geometric shapes cut out of Bristol board, could arouse no interest in his work— though he was in fact the initiator of experiments being taken up to-day with considerably more spirit, by the *avant-garde* of America. Similarly, the symphonic film, which in the works of Walter Ruttmann and Fischinger (*Opus IV*, *Komposition in Blau*, Berlin) was then finding such ready acclamation in Berlin, met with a poor reception in Paris. Mme Dulac produced several intelligently conceived pictorial sequences on works of Chopin and Debussy, *Disque 357*, *Thème et Variations* and so on, but the idea was never taken up.

At this moment, the French *avant-garde* took a new path, an entirely spontaneous movement, having no theorist to give it definite formulation, but even in 1927 heralding the English documentary school later to be formed by John Grierson.

The first impetus to the new movement came almost certainly with the showing in France, in the Ciné-Clubs, of the banned films of Pudovkin, Eisenstein and Dziga Vertov. Films like *The Mother*, or *Potemkin*, brought it forcefully home to the young French artists that there was more poetry to be found in the human face of the man in the street than in the mechanical objects and cut-out shapes of the abstract films, and greater art in good editing than in the laboured searching after poetic effect.

42

Significant indication of the new trend is the fact that in 1928 a gifted young director, Georges Lacombe, embarked on his first independent work (he had previously worked as assistant to René Clair). He went straight to the field of documentary, and his first film was about the Paris rag-and-bone men, recording in detail their searching of the dustbins, and the routine burning of the city's kitchen refuse.

Man and society returned as it were to the field of vision of the *avant-garde*. The young independent directors opened, or at least half-opened, their studio windows to life, and began to conceive of reality as a source of social subject-matter, not merely as a source of exotic settings. As further proof of the new trend, now signalized by Lacombe's success, came the first film of Marcel Carné, *Nogent, Eldorado du Dimanche*, a picture of the 'plage' on the banks of the Marne, Sunday resort of the Paris working-class, and the *Vendanges* of Georges Rouquier, the printer from the Languedoc, who was later to have such success with *Farrebique*. So strongly did the tide set in that the work of directors who had made their début with films in the style of the *Ballet Mécanique*, such as Deslaw, director of *Marche des Machines*, instead of going for the abstract, turned towards what might virtually be called Paris *reportage*, *La Nuit Electrique* and *Parnasse*.

The masterpiece of the *avant-garde* documentary was Jean Vigo's *A Propos de Nice*—a piece of violent, bitter social satire reflecting the influence both of Bunuel's Surrealism and of the theories of Dziga Vertov (whose brother and assistant, Boris Kaufman, acted as Vigo's camera-man). Here the wild festivities of the Carnival, the absurdities of an Italian cemetery, the pretentious statues of the big hotels, the fashionable women, the beggars, the pedigree lapdogs, viewed with ruthless exactitude, are contrasted with images, the more poignant because of the directness and depth of their meaning—laundry drying at the windows, dilapidated housefronts, slum dwellings, and sick and ragged children in the narrow streets of Old Nice.

Bunuel, for his part, turned to the other extreme. From Surrealist poetics he plunged into the most uncompromising social realism. On the morrow of the proclamation of the Spanish Republic, we find him bringing out *Terre Sans Pain*, about the wild country of the Hurdes, peopled with characters from Velasquez and Goya, beggars, and the sick. A child's coffin carried across ravines, a stream serving at once as bathing place for lepers, drain for refuse and source of drinking water,

43

stone hovels offering the barest and bleakest of shelter, starving goats nibbling leaves and twigs, children growing up on wild berries, cripples, cretins, goitre cases, monsters with fourteen toes—are all described with a rather sadistic pity, the misery of their lot recounted by the dispassionate, nicely-turned phrases of a commentator.

Thus the French *avant-garde* movement was turning into a school of documentary. Alongside Vigo and Bunuel, the ranks were swelled by newly-fledged directors—Carné, Rouquier, Grémillon, Lacombe. Jean Lods, also, who followed up an hour-by-hour diary of the Champs-Élysées with a film of the runner Ladoumègue breaking the mile record —and Jean Painlevé, the scientist, whose films of underwater life were real works of art.

Painlevé, son of a mathematician who had also figured in politics, began with a series of films on *La Pieuvre*, *Les Oursins*, *La Daphnie* and *Hyas* in which he showed himself still considerably under the influence of the abstract films. He dwelt in astonishment on the splendours to be found in a pool or a drop of water, on the likeness of these geometric patternings to those in the water paintings of Kandinski or Picasso. After 1930, however, Painlevé's work comes into closer relation with humanity. His 'animalcules' are no longer merely interesting shapes, but heroes. He endows them with individual lives, and becomes the Flaherty of the aquatic world, depicting the ferocity of *Bernard L'Hermite*, or the gracefulness, and the strange love story, of *L'Hippocampe*.

But this blossoming of the *avant-garde* into human and social documentary was checked. With the coming of the 'talkie', the costs of film production soared. To produce even a short sequence, if it were to have a sound-track, was no longer possible without much greater funds than the experimental studios had at their disposal. The days when Marcel Carné could produce *Nogent* on a few thousand francs were goné for ever. To add to the difficulties, the specialist cinemas were beginning to shun *avant-garde* work, and seeking their films of artistic or historical interest among the big foreign productions. Assistance from a few wealthy patrons, such as the Vicomte de Noailles (who financed *L'Age d'Or* and *Le Sang d'un Poète*), together with a return by some directors like Painlevé to the old methods whereby the director did nearly all the technical work himself, enabled the *avant-garde* to survive for a short period after the advent of the 'talkie'. But by 1930 economic crisis had broken up the movement. On the other hand, the men who had served their apprenticeship in the experimental studios were now brought out to direct big films for a wide public, and it was they who formed the nucleus of a movement which was a few years later to rise to the proportions of a renaissance of the French School in the cinema.

VI

JACQUES FEYDER, RENÉ CLAIR & THE CHANGE-OVER FROM THE SILENT TO THE TALKING FILM

1923—1931

IT must not be imagined that the work of the Impressionist school and the esoteric experimentation of the *avant-garde* represent the entire French film production of 1918–30. In spite of the continual slowing down of work in the studios, thousands of films were made in France over this period.

One of the most active production companies of the time was that of Ciné-Romans, founded and sponsored by the newspaper *Matin*, whose director, Sapène, liked to visualize himself as the W. Randolph Hearst of France. This lesser edition of *Citizen Kane* unsuccessfully attempted to win the heart of the public for his Suzanne Alexander, the actress Claudia Victrix. He made his company specialize in serials but never managed to equal the triumphs of the earlier *The Clutching Hand*. The serial film had undergone much change since the days of the latter, and hooded bandits in contemporary settings were now out of fashion. Diamant-Berger's serial version of *Les Trois Mousquetaires*, though most of the episodes were mediocre, had set the ciné-novel firmly on the path to historical, costume and retrospective subjects.

For the frankly commercial studios, adaptation remained the golden rule. French literature, past and present, provided an inexhaustible source of inspiration. Poirier and Baroncelli, for example, were directors whose whole output consisted of such films of adaptation.

Baroncelli's work included some films of real quality. His *Père Goriot*, while it does not succeed in bringing to the screen the full force and impetus of Balzac, reconstructs most effectively the dingy Vauquier boarding-houses. The same director was also responsible for *Nène*, after a novel that had just won the Prix Goncourt, *Pêcheurs d'Islande*, and *Ramuntcho* by Pierre Loti. There were passages in these films conveying a very real and vivid impression of the picturesque in peasant life, and the director has a fine feeling for landscape.

Léon Poirier, after a series of films inspired by the Arabian Nights, adapted first Lamartine's *Jocelyn*, and then a Prix Goncourt novel, *La Brière*. Out of this latter he created his best film, a camera description of a stretch of marshy country on the borders of Brittany that brings out all its natural grandeur and poetry; there are traces of Swedish influence here. The success of this study of Brittany headed Poirier in the direction of documentary. Joining an expedition organized as part of a publicity campaign by the motor manufacturer Citroen, he travelled the breadth of Africa, and brought back the material he worked into *Croisière Noire*—the film notebook of a tourist keenly alive to the picturesque and the exotic, the beauty of the forests, the styles of dwellings and the un-clothed natives. (A similar record of Africa was shortly afterwards brought back by the young Marc Allégret, who had been the travelling companion of André Gide. His series of charming sketches were obtained with equipment very much inferior to Poirier's.)

Poirier's next expedition was to Madagascar, where with one professional French actor and the aid of the natives, he embarked upon a version of the story of *Cain*. But this film was a failure. His documentary interest, however, persisted, finding evident expression in his next work, *Verdun, Vision d'Histoire*, an historical reconstruction on an enormous scale of the battle of 1916, preaching a pacifism à la Briand and a Franco-German rapprochement (in which he was in tune with the French foreign policy of the day). Poirier was not the only director at this period to turn to history. Henri Roussel bore him company with his *Violettes Impériales* and so did Raymond Bernard. Bernard, who had begun his career with adaptations from various successes of his father, the popular novelist Tristan Bernard, launched forth in 1924 with a chronicle film of the reign of Louis XI, *Miracles des Loups*, for one scene of which he

47

assembled a veritable army under the old medieval walls of Carcassonne. The finished film, authentic, polished and stately, with the right degree of pomp and splendour, was a great success in France and abroad. The director followed it up with another in the same historical style, *Joueur d'Échecs*, but this met with a less warm reception.

A name worth singling out from among the 'adaptor' directors is that of Henri Fescourt—who had served a pre-war apprenticeship with Gaumont under Louis Feuillade. His *Misérables* was one of the best of the film versions (ten in all) of Hugo's novel thus far produced since the origin of the cinema. Fescourt gave unmistakable proof here of taste and sensibility, of a lively feeling for beauty of image, and of rare discretion. Too much discretion, perhaps, for the establishment of a personal reputation. His *Monte Christo*, while it did not rise to the standard of *Les Misérables*, was nevertheless remarkable for the skilful ingenuity of its décor; great use was made of Schuftan effects, then still a novelty.

In the last few years of financial prosperity, French film production, in a movement to rival Hollywood, had been developing a strong tendency towards spectacular kinds of production with lavish costume and décor. And in search of the necessary financial backing, production companies turned to negotiation with international combines—a departure accompanied by a corresponding trend toward cosmopolitanism in French production.

French directors, in the days of Delluc, while eagerly studying foreign films, had remained, first and foremost, *French*, keen to the fact that their market was almost entirely a home one. The same period, after 1918, however, had seen the development in Paris of a foreign colony with a distinctive life of its own. It was the influential group of Russian emigrés —numbering among its members the actors Mosjoukine, Nathalie Kovanko, Nathalie Lissenko, Nicolas Koline, the directors Starevitch, Volkov, Protozanov, Tourjanski, and producers Ermolief and Alexander Kamenka.

This band of exiles lost little time in hiring studios and, with their own capital, setting up film production in France. Their first films were almost indistinguishable from those they had made earlier in Moscow or the Crimea. Then gradually their work, uprooted from the national soil, lost its peculiarly Russian character, took on a neutral, denationalized cosmopolitan flavour. Mosjoukine, the highly extravagant personality who dominated this Russian group, specialized in a sort of vaporous fantasy, imbued with a certain bitter romanticism, often clearly influenced by German expressionism, in films like *Kean*, adapted from Alexandre Dumas, *Le Lion des Mongols* directed by Epstein, and, especially, *Le Brasier Ardent*. Mosjoukine reached the height of his reputation —if not of his art—with his lavish *Casanova*, directed by Volkov and financed by a French-German combine.

Collaboration between Paris and Berlin was, in fact, developing apace. While America was colonizing the German cinemas, German financiers were attempting to do the same to the French and, indeed, to the European market, by producing films in which stars from Berlin or Paris rubbed shoulders with others from Rome, Vienna, Stockholm, or London. There was much talk of Europe and a European Cinema. The great majority of these cosmopolitan efforts were from the artistic point of view quite sterile. The exceptions were films created by the most authoritative French director up to 1930 along with Abel Gance— Jacques Feyder.

Feyder, born in Brussels, had come to Paris as early as 1914, his ambitions centred round the stage. He played a few minor roles; then, during the war, he became a director with Gaumont. His first essays in film-making were poor. But he leaped to sudden commercial success with *Atlantide*, an adaptation of a famous novel by Pierre Benoit, filmed several times subsequently. The novel is set in the Sahara, and Feyder, taking a unit and equipment to the desert, shot all the exteriors on the spot, with a fine sense of realism. Unfortunately, the interior scenes fail to maintain this realism. Made on sets erected by an Italian designer in a suburb of Algiers, they have all the oppressive over-lavishness that spoilt pre-war adaptations such as *Cabiria* or *Quo Vadis?* But, in spite of its imperfections, *Atlantide* must be given its due as one of the few post-1920 French productions to attract any attention abroad.

On an artistic level, Feyder's first important film was *Crainquebille*, adapted from Anatole France's famous novel, in which a barrow merchant, unjustly accused of having insulted a policeman, is sent to gaol, thereby losing his customers as well as the respect of the neighbourhood. This cinematographic short story, on the face of it so much less ambitious than *Atlantide*, would have passed unnoticed by *avant-garde* criticism, were it not for Feyder's introduction, in the court-room scene, of some ingenious trick effects in which the Méliès tradition is fused with the inspiration of German expressionism—showing, for example, a

49

diminutive Crainquebille overshadowed by a gigantic policeman. But the film was criticized on the two main counts that the director had chosen his basic story from the novel of an academician, and that he had called on a member of the Comédie Française to act in it. The critics, in fact, scented the film d'art.

None the less, *Crainquebille* has come to be regarded as one of the key works of the French cinema, since it represents the transition between the naïve pre-1914 realism of Zecca, Jasset and Feuillade, and the French school of pre-1940, in which a major part was to be played by a pupil of Feyder's, Marcel Carné. Griffith was making no mistake when, referring to *Crainquebille*, he declared to a journalist, 'I have seen a film that, for me, symbolizes Paris. That man with his barrowload of vegetables— what a striking image—and how forceful! And Féraudy—great, powerful acting! A fine work, beautiful, compelling, bold!'

Féraudy, who had played in or directed several films d'art, gave indeed an extraordinarily vivid performance as Crainquebille. Standing among many traders, in a poor and busy street, he seemed to have sprouted from the very paving-stones of Paris. These scenes from the life of the people have a powerful authenticity, bringing them close at times to certain Russian productions, and which heralds the coming of Jean Renoir through whose work they were to influence the neo-realist movement in Italy. Literary 'Zolaesque' naturalism was here given conscious and adequate film expression. Thanks to the generosity of Anatole France, at times *Crainquebille* achieves true realism especially in scenes containing a meaning deeper than mere picturesque description, or the impressionist rendering of events in the court-room.

Feyder, who had a natural gift for imbuing realism with poetry, met with less success when he attempted to distil this same poetic quality from more sophisticated and often over-literary scenarios. The film he himself, to the last, preferred of all his work was *L'Image*, written by Jules Romains.

Three men here fall in love with a single unknown woman, whose portrait they have seen in a photographer's window. They then all three find themselves together in Hungary, only a short distance from the château where this ideal woman lives in retirement from the world. But all three renounce the intention of seeing her, since each confesses that in his own mind he has formed an image of her very different from that of the others, and equally far removed from reality.

50

The somewhat rudimentary Pirandellism of this basic idea was developed with a scholastic kind of rigidity which makes the whole story seem to our eyes to-day very artificial; but at the time its ingenuity was greatly praised. The high place it occupied in Feyder's own affections was doubtless due to the incorporation in it of two themes constantly recurring in his work—ardent passion for a mysterious or unknown woman: *L'Atlantide, Carmen, Le Grand Jeu, La Loi du Nord*, and the gulf separating reality from the individual's own vision of it: *Crainquebille, Gribiche, Les Nouveaux Messieurs, La Kermesse Héroïque, Le Grand Jeu*. Another favourite theme of Feyder's, absent from *L'Image*, is that of maternal love, which found expression at this period in *Gribiche*, and especially *Visages d'Enfants*. He returned to it later in *Pension Mimosas*.

'A setting, an atmosphere, and a popular plot with a little melodrama in it.' Thus Feyder defined the ingredients of his art, and all his life he remained faithful to this formula. The scales were sometimes tipped a little too heavily towards melodrama and consequent sentimentality; *Gribiche*, for instance, is swamped by it, and one of his best films, *Visages d'Enfants*, made in Switzerland, among the landscape and picturesque costume of the Valais, is not entirely free from melodramatic overweight.

Jacques Feyder had a leaning towards precision and minute detail. This quality of temperament, guarantee of sound workmanship though it was, went as so often happens, with a certain coldness. But the latter is not so marked as to overshadow a very real love of life and men—observed in his work with great penetration, sometimes also with bitterness. This director was soon aware of the shackles production finance imposed upon his calling, and felt himself reined in. After *Carmen*, in the making of which he had struggled under the harsh, unreasonable handicap of a star, Raquel Meller, imposed upon him as a condition of production, he declared to his friend Moussinac, in a newspaper interview for *L'Humanité*, that he did not believe film-making could exist as an art in existing economic circumstances.

L'Image had been made in Hungary, *Visages d'Enfants* in Switzerland. *Thérèse Raquin* was directed in Berlin. Zola's novel is the story of a 'crime passionel'. Unhappily married to a sickly shopkeeper, the sensuous Thérèse persuades her lover to drown him. Then she installs the lover in the back-room of the shop, where lives also the paralysed, dumb mother of the murdered husband. The mother, an incarnation of reproach, finishes by killing the lovers. Though German actors and

51

technicians played a major role in its production, Feyder's film remains throughout profoundly French, and as faithful to Zola as *Crainquebille* had been to Anatole France. Greater emphasis is laid on the sexual factor than in the novel, but the film is far from disregarding the social element. The work throughout is dominated by the insidious presence of the décor, a passage lit by a pane of glass, in which is unfolded the drama of passions, but which reflects also the whole life of these perfectly drawn small shopkeepers. Gina Manès, the greatest actress in French cinema at this period, gives an unforgettable study as Thérèse Raquin.

This film, to borrow the expression Flaubert used of Mme Bovary, inspired something of the same feelings as 'an awful mouldiness, at the bottom of a cupboard'. After its completion, in search of a change of air, Feyder tackled the vaudeville of the boulevards with *Les Nouveaux Messieurs*. The original work of this name was that of De Flers and de Croisset, who had provided many similar successes in light comedy in Paris during the first thirty years of the century. The authors showed a secrétaire de syndicat corrupted by bourgeois privilege, who becomes a minister and acquires a stage-star for his mistress. Political life both in France and abroad furnished abundant examples during the period for such a character, and the satire, written humorously but without venom, was greatly applauded by the political Left. The film, however, was not passed by the censor, because Feyder had depicted a Deputy's dream in which he peopled the French Parliament with a galaxy of Degas ballerinas. With the unexpected social implications of the film thus forced upon him, Feyder, shocked and discouraged, left France forthwith, pinning better hopes on Hollywood.

While it can hardly be ranked as a masterpiece, *Les Nouveaux Messieurs*, the last of Feyder's silent films to be made in Europe, contains some excellent passages. The prologue takes the form of a satire of a theatre, with its wigs and its stout singers, and is the forerunner of René Clair's *Le Million* or the later *Les Enfants du Paradis*, in which theatre and film were contrasted in more serious vein. The best scenes of *Les Nouveaux Messieurs* recount the opening ceremony of a 'workers' city', in which dinner-jacketed politicians, hurrying because the fate of their ministry in Paris hangs precariously in the balance, run perfunctorily through their offices with the agitated speed of a news-reel in accelerated motion. The Parliament sequences also, made with the aid of a fine

52

reconstruction set, the work of Lazare Meerson, have grandeur and authenticity.

We are struck immediately by the close resemblance in the best passages of *Les Nouveaux Messieurs*, to some of the most famous films of René Clair. The relationship is one of coincidence rather than of specific influence, though it can be attributed in part to the common derivation from vaudeville of both *Les Nouveaux Messieurs* and so many of Clair's films.

René Clair, after the success of *Entr'acte*, the near-failure of *Voyage Imaginaire*, and his documentary *La Tour* of much-debated merit, had abandoned the *avant-garde* in favour of a more general public. He thus followed the tenet of Louis Delluc, 'The great masters of the screen are those who address themselves to the world at large'.

In the new field, the young director needed a little time to find his way. *La Fantôme du Moulin Rouge* was made along the same lines as *Paris Qui Dort*—fantastic events taking place against the everyday background of Paris. But the film was tedious, and a failure. Then came *La Proie du Vent*, an attempt at the dramatic adventure story, for which the director turned out to have but little talent. The ingenious reconstruction of an aeroplane crash, a dream, an episode where the camera takes the audience as it were into the head and heart of the hero, fail to redeem an extremely conventional story.

Then Clair, who had himself chosen the subject of *Proie du Vent*, agreed, without enthusiasm, to direct a screen adaptation of Labiche and Michel's famous vaudeville comedy, written at the close of the reign of Louis Phillipe, *Un Chapeau de Paille d'Italie*. There existed at the time, in intelligent film circles, a strong antipathy against cinema adaptations of plays and novels. But it was this contact with a work of traditional French vaudeville that revealed to René Clair the true direction of his own talent. And *Un Chapeau de Paille d'Italie* also won him his first big public.

Labiche's play was the pursuit of an Italian straw hat during a grotesque wedding. The comic puppets of this film, and the sustained verve with which they were activated recall that here again is the talented director of *Entr'acte*. The quaint characters are sketched with a delightful sureness of touch, and Clair contrived to translate so artfully the original puns and word-play into visual gags that he was able to dispense almost entirely with sub-titles. He transposed the period story and

53

costumes of nearly a century ago into the more contemporary nineteen-twenties and thereby rendered more ludicrous than ever the doings of the *petit-bourgeois* characters. Like the films of Méliès or Chaplin, *Un Chapeau de Paille d'Italie* evolves like a beautifully worked-out ballet, polished to the last degree of precision, elegant, coolly ironic, embroidering on an ingenious theme, bringing off the sudden rebounding comic effect with easy faultlessness of timing. A Lancers Quadrille, the best part of the film, is a model of rhythm and cutting, surpassing even the famous pursuit in *Entr'acte*. Other passages were almost as successful, typifying minor characters by such grotesque details as those of Chaplin's *The Cure* or *The Adventurer*. In this film Clair presents without venom but equally without mercy, a caricature of 'all the little phobias, the vexations, all the habits and extravagances, of the French *petite-bourgeoisie* at the turn of the century'.*

René Clair, with his same producer, Alexander Kamenka, tried to repeat their great success with another adaptation from Labiche, *Les Deux Timides*, centring round similar *petit-bourgeois* puppet characters as those of the *Chapeau de Paille*, the young marriageable daughter, the timid wooer, his blustering rival, and the father-in-law. But this time they were less successful. The scenario lacked backbone, and was burdened by a rather heavy-handed parody of the detective-story film.

Economic circumstances and technical development now combined to face René Clair suddenly with the problems of sound film. When the sound-track revolutionized the film industry, Clair was working on the script of a new film *Prix de Beauté*. This he altered in an attempt to meet the requirements of the new medium, then, discouraged, abandoned its direction to the Italian Genina. He declared himself, emphatically, the enemy of the sound-track, which indeed seemed both dangerous and useless to a director whose art, learnt from Feuillade and Chaplin, consisted of complete and precise visual expression *without* dialogue. Independent film criticism and the more artistically developed of the general film public were unanimously of Clair's opinion. But the force of a condemnation coming from an intellectual minority was powerless to stem the tide. In utter discouragement, Clair thought of abandoning work in films altogether and had the novel he published at this period, *Adams*, been the success for which he had hoped, he might well have devoted himself entirely to literature.

* Leon Moussinac.

This revolt, and the support it received, seems surprising to-day. It is more easily understood when one has seen the mediocrity of the first all-talking productions. In all of them the camera, shut off in an immobile sound-proof cabin, acts as a stationary recorder of an action taking place on a stage. Vaudeville, operettas, songs, operas and music-hall, take their turn, and not one of them is worth any consideration from an artistic point of view. The first French films in the new medium—*L'Eau de Nil; La Nuit est à Nous; La Route est Belle; Les Trois Masques* mostly made in London, French studios being not yet suitably equipped, were tremendous financial successes, but artistically they fall even below the level of *The Jazz Singer*, which served as their model.

Now that the film was seeking to deal with more complex sentiments and situations, the absence of sound and dialogue had been growing into a handicap. The Danish director Carl Dreyer, arriving in Paris to make his *Passion de Jeanne d'Arc*, to the consternation of opposers of the new technique, declared that he would prefer to work with the aid of the sound-track.

Though directed by a foreigner, *Jeanne d'Arc* is, by subject, actors and technicians, a French film—the exceptional nature of its art and style making it impossible to classify with the works of any other national school. The scenario included the speeches of Jeanne and her judges as garnered from historical documents, abridged and condensed only so far as was necessary in the interests of dramatic tension to shorten the duration of the trial to one day. The finest part of this admirable piece of work was the question-and-answer duel between Joan (Falconetti) and her inquisitors, led by Bishop Cauchon (Sylvain). Words here would have been of infinite value to the production—the series of sub-titles, which Dreyer was obliged to use, breaks up an otherwise perfect, harmonious continuity of images and cutting.

La Passion de Jeanne d'Arc was not an historical film in the sense in which this term had come to be applied. Imposing settings, and famous actors, played here a very small role; attention was focused rather on close-ups of human faces and figures, and significant objects. Make-up, wigs, and all other artificial aids to characterization were alike banned, and Dreyer managed to persuade his cast that they were actually living the story. Every movement of the lashes, every tear was an exact and faithful representation of reality. Every cracked lip, every grain of beauty, every wart, almost down to every pore, had its part to play in this staggering revelation of the powers of expression inherent in the countenance of man. Brought thus face to face with the characters, the spectator is drawn at once into the very centre of the drama—with an irresistibility, never achieved by tracking shot or 'camera in the first person'. Dreyer's film, in its presentation of the fifteenth century and the simple-hearted patriotism of the Maid, rises over and beyond particularities of time and individual characters to the heights of the universal in human experience. It was an achievement to the making of which had gone lessons learnt from the experiments of the German Kammerspiel and the great works issuing from Russia.

Jeanne d'Arc, unfortunately, has no successor. The second film Dreyer made in Paris, *Vampyr*, distinctly less French in its overtones and of a more hybrid character altogether, though it contains some remarkable passages—such as the famous portrayal of a burial scene seen from a coffin through the eyes of a dead man—was a failure.

Meanwhile, the success of the first talkies was attracting the attention of the businessman. Investors who had backed the early rapid rise to prosperity of Pathé and Gaumont, began to think in terms of the creation of a new monopoly around the old trade-names. Charles Pathé, his fortune made, had gone into retirement. The concern that bore his name was taken up by a speculator named Natan and subsequently emerged as the cartel Pathé-Natan-Cinéromans, sponsored by the banking firm of Bauer and Marshall. At the same time there came into being a parallel group, Gaumont-Aubert-Franco-Films, backed by the Crédit Industriel et Commercial and the Industrie Electrique Suisse. These two combines, possessing exhibition circuits, distribution agents, laboratories and studios, were the first to acquire sound-track equipment.

But the policy of deliberate liquidation of the French cinema industry, adopted by these Paris financiers during the years immediately following the war, made the establishment of new concerns difficult. France had now ceased to manufacture film celluloid, and she possessed no patent for sound. The numerous skilled French inventors of sound-recording methods for film (Lauste, Baron, and several others) having met with neither encouragement nor financial support at home, had either sold their patents abroad or abandoned research altogether. All the rights of the new technique, now ripe for commercial exploitation, were in the hands of two big international organizations, Western of America and

56

THE FLIGHT OF A BIRD
a series of photographs made by Marey, round 1887

Lumière's Cinematograph showing at the Empire, Leicester Square, London. (Photograph from a Lumière film, 1896)

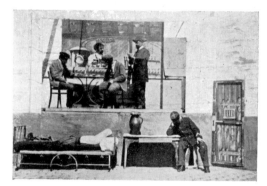

HISTOIRE D'UN CRIME
(F. Zucca) 1901

VOYAGE À LA LUNE
(Georges Méliès) 1902

L'ASSASSINAT DU DUC
DE GUISE
(Le Bargy and Calmettes)
1908

NICK CARTER
(Victorin Jasset) 1908

ONÉSIME
(Jean Durand) 1912-14

MAX LINDER
IN LE PETIT CAFÉ
1919

SARAH BERNHARDT IN
MÈRES FRANÇAISES
(Mercanton) 1916

JUDEX
(Louis Feuillade) 1916

LA FEMME DE NULLE PART
(Louis Delluc) 1922

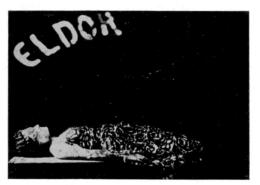

ELDORADO
(Marcel l'Herbier) 1922

MONTE CHRISTO
(Pouctal) 1917

LA ROUE
(Abel Gance) 1922

MME BEUDET
La Souriante
(Germaine Dulac) 1923

NAPOLÉON
(Abel Gance)
1927

LES DEUX
TIMIDES
(René Clair)
1928

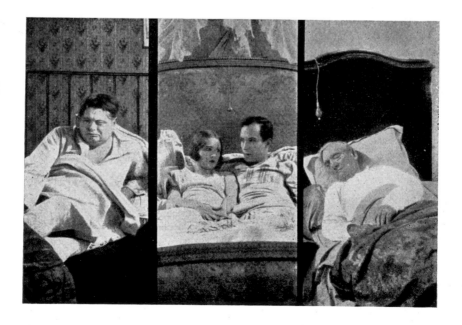

LES DEUX TIMIDES
(René Clair) 1928

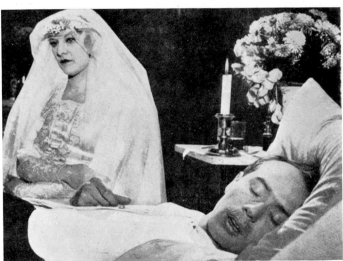

THÉRÈSE RAQUIN
(Jacques Feyder) 1928

LES NOUVEAUX
MESSIEURS
(Jacques Feyder) 1929

THE SEASHELL AND THE CLERGYMAN
(Germaine Dulac)   1928

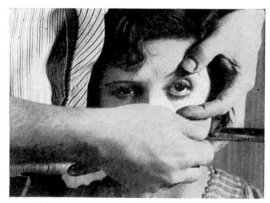

UN CHIEN ANDALOU
(Luis Bunuel)   1928

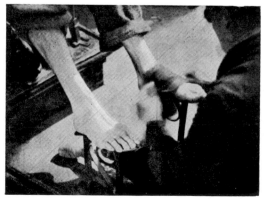

À PROPOS DE NICE
(Jean Vigo)   1929

CRAINQUEBILLE
(Jacques Feyder)   1923

LA PASSION DE JEANNE D'ARC
(Carl Dreyer) 1928

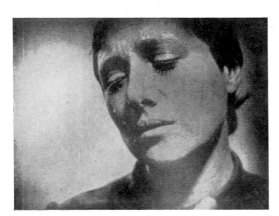

LA PASSION DE JEANNE D'ARC
(Carl Dreyer) 1928

UN CHAPEAU DE
PAILLE D'ITALIE
(René Clair) 1927

MÉNILMONTANT
(Dimitri Kirsanov) 1928

MALDONE
(Jean Grémillon) 1928

ZÉRO DE CONDUITE
(Jean Vigo) 1932

L'ATALANTE
(Jean Vigo)   1934

L'AFFAIRE EST DANS LE SAC
(Pierre Prévert)

ENTR'ACTE
(René Clair)   1924

LE MILLION
(René Clair)   1931

À NOUS LA LIBERTÉ
(René Clair) 1932

QUATORZE JUILLET
(René Clair) 1933

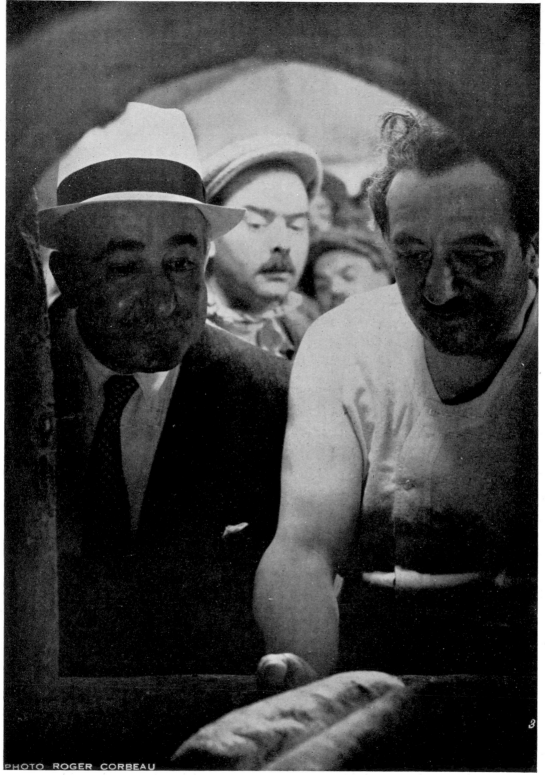

LA FEMME DU BOULANGER
(Marcel Pagnol)   1938

POIL DE CAROTTE
(Julien Duvivier) 1925

LA BANDERA
(Julien Duvivier) 1935

LES DISPARUS DE ST. AGIL
(Christian-Jaque) 1938

QUAI DES BRUMES
(Marcel Carné) 1938

LE JOUR SE LÈVE
(Marcel Carné) 1939

LE CRIME DE MON. LANGE
(Jean Renoir) 1935

LA MARSEILLAISE
(Jean Renoir) 1938

LA GRANDE ILLUSION
(Jean Renoir) 1938

LA BÊTE HUMAINE
(Jean Renoir) 1938

LA RÈGLE DU JEU
(Jean Renoir) 1939

LA BELLE EQUIPPE
(Julien Duvivier)   1936

ESPOIR
(André Malraux)   1939

L'HIPPOCAMPE
(Jean Painlevé) 1934

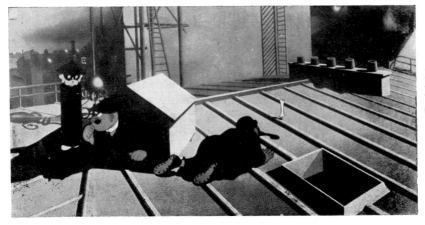

LE VOLEUR DE
PARATONNERRES
(Paul Grimault) 1946

LUMIÈRE D'ÉTÉ
(Jean Grémillon) 1942

LES VISITEURS DU SOIR
(Marcel Carné) 1942

LA NUIT FANTASTIQUE
(Marcel l'Herbier) 1942

L'ETERNEL RETOUR
(Jean Delannoy) 1943

DOUCE
(Claude Autant-Lara) 1943

LES ANGES DU PÉCHÉ
(Robert Bresson) 1943

NOUS LES GOSSES
(Lous Daquin) 1941

LA BATAILLE DU RAIL
(René Clément) 1945

FARREBIQUE
(Georges Rouquier) 1946

LES PORTES DE LA NUIT
(Marcel Carné) 1946

OCCUPE-TOI D'AMÉLIE
(Claude Autant-Lara)   1949

LA BELLE ET LA BÊTE
(Jean Cocteau)   1946

JOUR DE FÊTE
(Jacques Tati)   1949

LE VOYAGE SURPRISE
(Pierre Prévert)   1946

LE POINT DE JOUR
(Louis Daquin) 1949

GOUPI MAINS ROUGES
(Jacques Becker) 1943

ANTOINE ET ANTOINETTE
(Jacques Becker) 1947

LE CORBEAU
(H. G. Clouzot)   1943

QUAI DES ORFÈVRES
(H. G. Clouzot)   1947

MANON
(H. G. Clouzot)   1949

LE SILENCE EST D'OR
(René Clair) 1947

LE DIABLE AU CORPS
(Claude Autant-Lara) 1947

LA BEAUTÉ DU DIABLE
(René Clair) 1949

UNE SI JOLIE PETITE PLAGE
(Yves Allegret) 1948

the German firm Tobis—both of them tied up with the big electrical industry.

The French firms had thus to pay out enormous sums to acquire the rights of sound-track cinema equipment. That used by the Western company, most generally favoured, cost at that time no less than 800,000 francs (£8,000 in pre-1940 sterling). But hundreds of cinemas accepted the draconian conditions—and Hollywood bled the French cinema industry to the tune of millions of dollars.

French and Americans now set up production in Paris almost simultaneously, in the studios of Tobis and Paramount respectively. Paramount, installed in the suburbs at Joinville le Pont, planned to create a European Hollywood. To the stipulations of producers and directors frankly and aggressively Californian there was constructed one gigantic film factory, that rapidly assumed the character of a tower of Babel. Some of the films that emerged therefrom were made in no fewer than fourteen or fifteen different linguistic versions. Overall scenarios, in which details of dialogue were of no importance, were used for these mass-produced pictures. The same scenes of the same film were played successively, on the same sets, by actors brought from France, Holland, Sweden, Denmark, Spain, Portugal, Czechoslovakia, Poland, Rumania, Hungary, Germany, Yugoslavia, Greece, Egypt, Lithuania, under a director who might or might not be of their own nationality. Subjects were chosen for the cosmopolitanism of their appeal, and determined preference accorded to those whose setting was in the salon or the night-club—cheap and easy sets to build, and dress with an air of apparent luxury. By such means, Paramount raked in the major profits from all the European markets, as well as those of Africa and Latin-America. But though this company had on its pay-roll some men of no little talent—Marcel Pagnol, Marcel Achard, Alexander Korda, Alberto Cavalcanti—nothing could be worse than these mass-produced Paramount canned-goods. The more artistically endowed directors, indeed, could not stand the ruthlessly commercial pace; a number of them crossed to England, there to take up again, sometimes with brilliant results, careers compromised in Paris.

Tobis adopted more prudent tactics than their rival firm. Berlin was geographically close enough to Paris for it to be a relatively simple matter to gather there, under a few weeks' contract, in another 'land of Babel', the actors, technicians, and directors needed to make any French version. On these lines, Tobis produced a series of films, numerically few by comparison with the output of Paramount, but directed with a certain regard for quality, both in the nature of box-office appeal and artistic standards. The French version of Pabst's *Drei Gröschen Opera*, for example, *L'Opéra de Quat'sous*, with Albert Préjean, Florelle and Margo Lion, was very nearly the equal of the German original.

At the same time, Tobis opened a big studio at Epinay, near Paris, where films were produced with the same regard for quality, that, save in the matter of their financial backing, were entirely French. The first production to come from this studio was a rare artistic event and a resounding success—René Clair's *Sous les Toits de Paris*.

Clair had by now resigned himself to the inevitability of the sound-track, but was still far from joining the ranks of its supporters, and in some ways *Sous les Toits de Paris* suggests a satire of the sound medium. The glass-panel door that slams to before certain of the characters just as they are about to speak is in this respect something of a symbol. The dialogue is poor, and the director has sometimes failed to perceive the irrelevancy of some of the old silent-film conventions. Midnight, for example, is announced, not by the striking of a clock, but by super-imposition of a clock-face on the décor. On the other hand, he has followed the theories of Eisenstein and Pudovkin in bold but naïve experiments in sound counterpoint. But these defects, inevitable accompaniments of a first film in the new medium, are minor ones only. They are forgotten in remembering the delightful whole, a direct and vivid evocation of the charm of Paris. The story, the loves of a street-singer, is ordinary enough. But Clair, with the aid of some fine sets by Lazare Meerson, realistic and poetic at the same time, have succeeded in recapturing enchantingly the atmosphere of the Paris suburb—the furnished rooms, the children playing, the crotchety concièrges, the window boxes, the idlers, the small shop-keepers, the respectable youths and the less so, the street-singers with their accordion in every square. Perhaps because it is such a faithful picture of that city, the film attracted little interest in Paris itself. But in Berlin it was greeted with scenes of unprecedented enthusiasm, which were to be repeated all over Europe and America—and even in Japan, where, it is said, its popularity has still to show signs of waning. It was revived in 1946 in Occupied Germany and Tokio, and met with renewed acclamation. Thus the 'popular' tradition, inaugurated by Zecca and Jasset, and handed on via Feuillade to the young Clair who had worked as his assistant, had led up to a great international success. Yokohama, Buenos Aires, Hamburg, applauded alike the exoticism that for them surrounded a Parisian *faubourg* street-singer, the deep humanity and understanding of the people, and the tenderness and the optimism that the film breathed. Delluc's theories were proved well-founded. A film at once *cinema* and *French*, combining technical virtuosity with true national character, conquered the great international public.

Unhappily, *Sous Les Toits de Paris* is the one exception among a host of second- and third-rate productions. Paramount, Pathé Natan, Gaumont Aubert, reinforced by a few independents, seemed to combine in a joint effort to swell the stream of commercial mediocrity. But Clair's film comes like an early swallow, harbinger of a now not-too-distant spring.

VII

THE FRENCH CINEMA SUFFERS FROM THE DEPRESSION

THE public's infatuation for French-speaking films stimulated Parisian production. From a total of 52 feature films in 1929, output jumped to 94 in 1930, to 130 in 1931 and to 157 in 1932. But this period of prosperity was short-lived. The economic depression which already had a firm grip on Germany and the English-speaking countries, now extended its stranglehold to France—a France which had just been tasting the golden fruits of victory, a country which had vested its national pride in its luxury and elegance, its rich cuisine and its refinement of living; which had come to accept as a matter of course homage to its achievements in literature and the arts, respect for its automobile industry, its armaments production, and the high exchange value of the franc. To such a country unemployment had seemed as remote an evil as the plagues of Egypt. But suddenly there were beggars in rags, making the rounds of empty cafés forsaken by the tourists. Poverty sprang up in the very midst of plenty; fear and anxiety assailed the minds of Frenchmen.

Le Million of René Clair, buoyant with its joyous fanfares and dancing cavalcades, came as the last major production of the carefree period. Like *Un Chapeau de Paille*, *Le Million* was adapted from a vaudeville comedy. The hero is a penniless Bohemian to whom salvation seems to be in winning a lottery ticket, but who realizes that his good fortune has really escaped him. René Clair spared no effort over this film, with its careful dialogue, and its song-and-dance numbers, a convention dating from Labiche, but given a new lease of popular life by German operetta films such as *Die Drei von der Tankstelle* and *Le Chemin du Paradis*.

60

Of all Clair's films, *Le Million* is probably the most perfect. Around the central theme the episodes and sequences unfold with a formal symmetry almost comparable to French classical architecture. The stout tenor, the enormous, flighty *prima donna*, the second-hand dealer, the bailiff, the taxi-driver, the chorus of tradesmen, the dwarf clerk, the foolish staring women, the idiot in bowler hat and breeches—all these puppet figures, drawn in deft, ironic caricature, are brought together in a dazzling, delightful farandola executed with the precision and exactitude that bears the imprint of René Clair.

In his next film, however, *A Nous la Liberté*, the carefree mood is relegated to the background. This work is the most ambitious of all Clair's films, and the one which makes greatest pretensions to depth and significance. Economic crises and unemployment had presented this generation with new and fundamental problems. *A Nous la Liberté*, inspired by the true life history of Charles Pathé, is the story of a one-time tramp who amasses a fabulous fortune as a manufacturer of photographic material. The idea of the opening sequence may also have been suggested to Clair, as a great admirer of Chaplin, by *The Gold Rush*. The hero, having become a big industrialist, is ironically, but with considerable truth to life, faced with the problems of mechanized production, monotonous labour and rationalization. The last reels depict a charming Utopia, a pleasing enough ending to the film but an inadequate solution to the problems it raises, in which the workers no longer work, but sit idly by, while the machines do all the work, and the boss returns to his first profession of tramp.

With its inadequate solution of social problems, Clair's film was none the less a clear sign of the times. It has many times been cited as forerunner of Chaplin's *Modern Times*. Dr. Goebbels, when he took control of Tobis, attempted for political reasons and in spite of the efforts of Clair, to bring a case against Chaplin for infringement of copyright. It has less often been observed how closely this film resembles later productions of Capra. The industrialist reverting to tramp for his own happiness and the good of all is brother to the ocarino-playing multimillionaire of *You Can't Take It With You*.

'*A Paris, dans chaque faubourg . . .*', the charming, lingering song with music by Georges Auric was the keynote of *Quatorze Juillet*, a film that conveys to perfection the spirit of the French national celebration, with the crowds in the squares, the dances, lanterns, accordions.

Unfortunately, the film does not keep within the limits of the title, but drags uselessly on through a rambling story of evil youths and the underworld.

Le Dernier Milliardaire was perhaps a more ambitious film than *A Nous la Liberté*. Setting his scene in Casinario, a fictitious country modelled in many respects on Monte Carlo, Clair attempted to depict an economic crisis and its outcome in political dictatorship. A barter system replaces coinage, and the price of a ham is paid in eggs; straw hats are taken out to sea and dumped overboard to get rid of a production surplus; and the mad dictator orders his ministers to cut off the legs of their trousers and proceeds to carry out a knee-inspection on all fours. The film contains a few comic passages worthy of comparison with Chaplin's *The Dictator*. But on the whole *Le Dernier Milliardaire* is disappointing. It lacks audacity, perhaps, and the deficiency is felt all the more because the acting is often weak. The film had a reception worse than it deserved. The failure may be partly attributed to the fact that the work, originally a Tobis production, was abandoned by that company when Dr. Goebbels took over its control, on the grounds that it was injurious to the Führer.

René Clair, discouraged, accepted the proposals made to him by Alexander Korda. He went to England to make his next film, *The Ghost Goes West*, which belongs more to the history of British cinema than to the French. Clair's exile was to last some twelve years. And his absence was the more grievously felt in France because his departure coincided with the death of a director on whom the country's film industry had placed great hopes, Jean Vigo.

Vigo was the son of an anarchist executed during the war by the Clemenceau government. A childhood spent in sordid provincial schools provided inspiration for his first film, *Zéro de Conduite*, which was for ten years banned by the censor. The work is a story in time, a bestowing of confidences, a portrait of the artist as a child. Its descriptions are vividly realistic; the influence of the Chaplin of *A Dog's Life* is very marked in this account of another sort of dog's life. Elsewhere in the film Vigo shows a true poetic lyricism—notably in the account of the revolt of the children against their adult oppressors, a symphony in white of nightshirts, sheets and feathers twisting in slow motion.

This first essay was followed by Vigo with *L'Atalante*. The theme here was one of more general interest, but the script, thrust upon the director, was weak. The lyrical passages of the film, where Vigo tried to introduce a note of fantasy, are a little overweighed with poetic, Surrealist encumbrances, and have not the directness and attraction of the great white storm in the closing scenes of *Zéro de Conduite*. The best passages are those set in the tumbledown, picturesque cabin of an eccentric sailor vividly acted by Michel Simon. One never forgets this singular setting, with its assortment of second-hand furnishings, the oppressive presence of the cats, and the sudden discovery in a cupboard of two amputated hands in a jar of alcohol.

The importance of *L'Atalante* lies in its revival of the tradition of the popular subject in the film, a tradition popular also at this time with René Clair, and the astonishing quality of poetry it engenders from a world superficially ordinary and drab. The theme of the film is the life of a man and wife on a barge whose name is the Atalante—the country wedding, awkward and touching, on the bank of the canal and the lockgates which for the girl suddenly open the road to Paris. The drama unfolds in the dramatic vista of an indeterminate waste land, the railway sidings in the industrial outskirts of Paris, dominated by steely electric pylons. Through this landscape, the barge seems to follow a set course which is symbolically the predestined course of the French tradition, a tradition which Marcel Carné observed and which set the fashion for the whole pre-1940 school.

Vigo, however, was far from having realized his full powers when death carried him off at the age of twenty-nine—a director worn out, like Delluc, in the struggle to create a French school in the cinema.

The emergence of such a school seemed still, at this time, remote. The mere quantitative increase in film production only meant greater opportunities for second-rate work in the industry. The most sought-after stars of the day were Milton, a mediocre artiste from music-hall, who could lay claim at best to the merits of a certain robust and popular verve, or the insipid Henri Garat, a veritable mannequin for the house of fashion, who looked dashing in evening clothes and murmured romantic words.

The French film, even on the commercial level, was at a loss for a road to follow. The public had had enough of mass-produced, meaningless *divertissements*. First nights at the Paramount cinema of their regular productions were becoming the occasion of protest, and even of disturbances. The American firm realized that it was time to withdraw. Production of multi-lingual films was abandoned, directors and chief technicians were recalled to the United States, personnel dismissed, and contracts liquidated. But Hollywood remained none thè less a powerful competitor in the French market. The Joinville studios were transformed into *dubbing* workshops, in which selected actors and actresses lent their voices to Greta Garbo, Shirley Temple or Clark Gable in Hollywood productions. The technique of dubbing, weak at first, rapidly improved; while at the same time the Parisian *élite* developed a taste for the original sub-titled version. The French film industry sought governmental protection.

Instead of the British 'quota' system, the French Government adopted a system of allocation based on measures formerly applied in Germany. A limit was set to the number of dubbed films that might be brought into the country—180, of which 120 were American—and the exhibition circuit of sub-titled works was restricted to ten or twelve cinemas. Foreign films made in France, or French films made abroad, were subjected to no restrictions. In the latter facilities the Americans displayed little interest, but Germany, on the other hand, exploited them to the full, and so, to a lesser degree, did Italy. The régimes of Hitler and Mussolini found the well-known French stars useful box-office attractions for films the profits of which were to help finance their projected war.

Apart from the work of Clair and Jean Vigo, the main production of French films during the first years of the sound-track yielded little of any real value. The advent of the new technique resulted in the retirement, or at least the temporary indisposition, of rising directors of the impressionist movement or the *avant-garde*—Marcel Carné, Jean Rouquier, Claude Autant-Lara, Luis Bunuel, Cavalcanti, Germaine Dulac, Jean Epstein, Marcel L'Herbier. Such successful productions as emerged seemed to happen by chance, isolated achievements whose promise was never sustained.

Such a film, for instance, was Jean Choux's *Jean de la Lune*, a delightful, popular story by Marcel Achard, acted to perfection by Michel Simon, René Lefèvre and Madeleine Renaud. There was a possible point of departure here for a series of French light comedies—with which the French might have preceded the work in this vein of Lubitsch and Capra in Hollywood. Marc Allégret, for example, the director of taste and intelligence who had made the successful *Mamzelle Nitouche*, a vaudeville in out-dated costume, and *Lac Aux Dames* with its discovery of Simone Simon and Jean-Pierre Aumont, might have found here ideal material for his talents. And at this same period Pierre and Jacques Prévert pointed the way to a new style of comedy with their excellent *avant-garde* film, *L'Affaire Est Dans le Sac*.

But possibly the economic situation was not conducive to the production of light films. We see how Georges Lacombe, for instance, a director with several average-standard comedies to his credit, turned with *Jeunesse*, a film remarkable for the quality of its observation, to the portrayal of the life of the working-class youth of Paris, in all its mean, unbroken hopelessness. And under the influence of the German naturalist movement another newcomer to film, Pierre Chenal, drove deliberately with his camera, in *Rue Sans Nom*, into the evil and the tragic style, depicting the down-at-heels and the rejects of society, and followed this film with a quasi-expressionist adaptation of *Crime and Punishment* (in which he directed Harry Bauer and Pierre Blanchar). The same note of despair, and the same preoccupation with criminals and wastrels, elements which stemmed from the naturalist tradition and characterized also one of the best of the early 'talkies', Jean Grémillon's *La Petite Lise*.

After *Tour au Large*, this young *avant-garde* director had sought a more general audience with *Maldone*, a film of somewhat melodramatic plot (written by Alexandre Arnoux for the actor Charles Dullin), but in which Grémillon's real quality as a director was readily apparent. *Gardien de Phares*, his next work, was a dramatic study of the conflict between two isolated lighthousekeepers made in the documentary style with a high degree of tension. It showed his talent developing apace, and with *La Petite Lise*, a naturalistic drama involving an escaped convict and a prostitute, Grémillon came into full realization of his powers. This film, which included some notable experiments in sound counterpoint, confirmed his position as one of the men of promise in the French school. Commercially, however, *La Petite Lise* was a failure, and the director was obliged to take a minor technical job in order to live. In the pursuit of his career he became for some years an exile.

Another film of this period that merits attention is Kirsanov's *Rapt*— an intelligent, curious work, embodying sound-track experiments analogous to those of Grémillon. Kirsanov, a director on the fringe of the *avant-garde*, had already to his credit, in *Ménilmontant*, an almost perfect film—in which this Russian director conveys more completely than any French contemporary, Clair excepted, the charm and poetry of the suburbs. *Rapt*, like *La Petite Lise*, was a commercial failure, and Kirsanov had perforce to make his next films with a more careful eye to the box-office, or abandon his profession altogether.

A like fate almost overtook Jean Renoir. The son of the great impressionist painter, he came to the cinema with all the advantages of the rich amateur. He founded his own production company, and was able, from his own resources, to finance *Nana*, a film he visualized as a luxurious international production, and in which the famous German actors Werner Krauss and Valenska Gert played side by side with the director's friend Jean Angélo, and his wife Catherine Hessling. Rich in its combination of the pictorial inheritance of impressionism and the realism of Zola's naturalist tradition, and drawing its inspiration also in part from the films of von Stroheim and the German school, *Nana* was one of the best French films of the later twenties, and the public received it with enthusiasm.

Unfortunately Renoir was no businessman. His film success was also his near financial ruin. He resigned himself to making commercial films, with an exception of *La Petite Marchande d'Allumettes*, partly from necessity, and partly also in an attempt to learn, by these despised methods, how the heart of the general public was to be won (*Tire au Flanc*, *Tournoi Dans la Cité*, and *Le Bled*).

The arrival of sound put him out of a job.

Then a chance success, *On Purge Bébé*, enabled him to make a film which marks a turning point in his work, *La Chienne* adapted from a novel by La Fouchardière, later adapted also by Fritz Lang in the film *Scarlet Street*. The plot, in no way remarkable, develops with the aid of old theatrical devices (a miscarriage of justice, sudden recognitions, a supposed return from the dead) a situation many times treated by the German film movement—the ruin of a respectable *petit bourgeois* in his fifties following fortune's malevolent introduction of him to a prostitute. But around this plot and its timeworn situations Jean Renoir built up, with a rare sureness of vision, a picture of Montmartre where the respectable middle classes and the racketeers live in immediate proximity. He conveys the nature of his characters via their *milieu*—the hero, for instance, a bank clerk (acted by Michel Simon), is introduced to us by way of his dingy, paltry apartment, with the sound of the child laboriously practising her scales next door. Michel Simon played the part superbly, and the stupid prostitute was well acted also by Junie Mareze, an actress who died not long afterwards.

Renoir had already developed his ability to get the most out of his actors, at least from those who were playing roles in which he was genuinely interested. But the acting of other roles in *La Chienne* was poor; as it was also in the director's next film, *Boudu Sauvé des Eaux*, an adaptation of a popular play about a wretched loafer who is befriended by a bookseller of the quais and in turn abuses his benefactor's generosity. Michel Simon's playing of the title role is not uniformly convincing because the director allowed him to overact the part. This production, imbued with an almost anarchist spirit, was technically of very uneven quality, and its commercial failure was complete. Since *La Chienne* was not a very profitable undertaking financially, Renoir was now again obliged to work 'to order', or with material not of his choosing, in *La Nuit du Carrefour*, *Chotard et Compagnie* and *Mme Bovary*.

It seemed that this time nothing could redeem him from the pit into which he had fallen in spite of himself. Indeed, he appeared to be sinking in even deeper, when it was announced that he was to make his next film for Marcel Pagnol.

The playwright Pagnol had achieved both fame and fortune as the creator of *Topaze*, a study, not profound but bold and striking, of a municipal councillor who succumbs to corruption. He possessed that fortunate ability, so rare in drama and literature, to create a *type*. When the talkie film was established, Pagnol became enthusiastic, declaring that now at last dramatic authors might be able to preserve great plays. This hope provoked general and violent protest from independent film critics who, in bitter memory of the wearisome and theatre-bound early talkies, believed the drama to be the worst possible enemy of the film. Their natural indignation obscured their realization that Pagnol, although mixing his ideas up with some provoking nonsense, was nevertheless making some intelligent suggestions, which, had they been taken up, might have enlisted the film camera in the service of drama to good purpose—well before the days of *Henry V* or *Les Parents Terribles*. Pagnol himself refrained from putting his ideas into practice. His first two films, *Marius* and *Fanny*, were received by the critics with a chorus of indignation.

These two plays had been 'canned', not by their author, but by Alexander Korda in the case of *Marius* and by Marc Allegret in the case

67

of *Fanny*. Pagnol had had, however, a considerable say in their method of shooting. Their technique is mediocre and flat, and does not come up to the level of the talented acting of Orane Demazis, Raimu, Pierre Fresnay, Charpin and Maupi. But the films owe to Pagnol's influence the detail and truthfulness of their settings. Their location-work vividly captures the atmosphere of Marseilles, here portrayed both accurately and picturesquely. The enthusiasm of the public was immense—and a great actor, Raimu, was given to the French cinema. Twenty years later these two films are still in considerable demand in France, Britain and elsewhere. As long afterwards as 1949, *Marius* achieved a great success with the intelligentzia of New York.

This transposition to the screen of a French theatrical tradition, whatever the view taken of it at the time, was a step of some importance. *Marius* brought to the cinema a theme which had occupied a major place in French literature since the end of the war—one theme of escape, of the attraction of lands unexplored, the lure of adventure. And Pagnol's two films had the merit also of proving, at a period when the general trend in commercial films was for subjects of cosmopolitan intrigue, that the exact, careful depiction of a national, even a provincial setting and characters, might prove an international success. And further, they brought home the importance of well-written dialogue, a matter in which even René Clair had not been over-critical. Such virtues outweigh the very evident faults of Pagnol, his over-facility, his readiness to use sentimental and outworn dramatic situations (the child-mother), and the rather too sharp business sense that caused him to push to the limit his formula of 'canned drama'. When Paramount, producer of his first films, liquidated its French company, he established on his own account a small workshop-studio in the suburbs of Marseilles, and there undertook, seemingly, the 'canning' of the whole French theatrical repertoire with plays like *Le Voyage de Monsieur Perrichon* and *Le Gendre de Monsieur Poirier*.

Pagnol studied his profession of film producer with an increasing enthusiasm. Using his own original and specially written scenarios, he found his work enjoying a growing success. There followed *Merlusse*, a good picture of the life of a provincial school-teacher (Pagnol's own profession hitherto), and then *Joffroy*, a short film in the true tradition of the *fabliaux*, in which an old peasant who has sold his field tries to keep both it and the money, in spite of the consternation and protests of the village. The southern sparkle of this film, its lively characterization and the beauty of the Provençal countryside, brought it very close to perfection. But this Pagnol did reach in *Angèle*, in which the daughter of a provincial farmer who has been seduced is saved from prostitution by a simple farm labourer. The theme of *Angèle* is a slender one, and the very real merit of the film lies in its interpretation and in the quality of its observation. In the tradition of Balzac, the countryside, the fittings, indeed all the accessories contribute to the social characterization of the film. Orane Demazis, notable as *Fanny*, gives an amazing performance as *Angèle*, and the acting of Fernandel surpasses even this.

Fernandel came, like Raimu, and a whole group of Pagnol's actors, from the Marseillaise music-hall. He had begun his film career with Jean Renoir, making his début in *Tire au Flanc*, and acquiring a name for himself with the public in *Adémai Aviateur*. In the latter film he partnered Noël-Noël, the charming exponent of comic nuance who came from Montmartre cabaret, and who created in *Adémai* a new kind of vaudeville trouper which succeeded with the public, becoming one of the few successful ventures in French comic types between the wars. After *Adémai Aviateur*, Fernandel descended to commercial comedy, where abuse was made of his talent and his horsy appearance. Critics were surprised to discover, in *Angèle*, that as a straight actor he could reach real dramatic, even tragic, power. *Angèle* remains Marcel Pagnol's finest film.

With Vigo's death, and the departure overseas of René Clair, it seemed that the economic crisis delivered its final blow to the French cinema. In 1934, production dropped from the 160 level of preceding years to 120. Amid confusion and dismay the industry saw its two most stalwart pillars, Pathé and Gaumont, topple and fall.

That enterprising man of business Bernard Natan, in the days before he controlled the Pathé group, had worked as a director and actor in films of an unquestionably pornographic kind. His activities in this direction had in fact earned him several months in gaol. When he subsequently reached heights of power in the industry, and a leading politician conferred upon him, at a banquet, the Légion d'Honneur, his numerous hostile rivals threatened to dig up the compromising past. But Natan, so the story goes, had taken adequate precautions; he informed the Head of Police, Chiappe, that in the event of a campaign against him, Pathé Journal, the weekly film paper which he controlled, would publish in all its editions an already prepared report on the slums of Paris. The counter-threat of uncovering these festering sores of society saved him from the threat of scandal.

It was not Natan's past that ruined him, but his present. By clever use and abuse of his holdings, he had, by astute juggling of the accounts, embezzled several millions of francs. He probably did not enjoy personally all the fruits of his swindling, but the responsibility was his. Once more he went to prison. The immense Pathé-Natan company was declared bankrupt. Its production, formerly so impressive, came to a standstill. The optimistic ending of that pleasant fable of René Clair's, *A Nous la Liberté*, was grievously belied in this real-life story—the more so as his term in prison proved to be, owing to the coming of war, an ante-chamber to the oven of the crematorium.

Gaumont also was losing its foothold. Financial difficulties accumulated, and the threads of a thousand speculative intrigues were woven about the impending crash. Tobis sought to absorb this great combine, which was still of major importance in France, though it now had little connection with its foreign offshoots. The struggle of conflicting interests took on a brutal tone, causing one notorious suicide. In the end Gaumont was saved from bankruptcy by the intervention of a large bank, the B.N.C.I., acting on behalf of the State.

The wind of panic blew coldly through the French film industry. Yet Paris, only a few years earlier, had been a refuge, both economic and political, to foreigners. Various financial combines had been formed, with big capital resources, to make *La Dame de Chez Maxim's* and *Le Roi Pausole*, directed by the Russian emigré Granowski, Fritz Lang's *Liliom* and Pabst's *Don Quixote*. These productions, made over-lavishly, with all kinds of extravagance, were not financially successful. Pabst, Lang and Erich Pommer, after a short period in Paris, all left for Hollywood, and Alexander Korda embarked upon a fruitful career in London. There remained in Paris only a few directors and businessmen, none with any great enthusiasm or enterprise. Denunciations began to be made of aliens who were thought to be keeping French film workers out of jobs, and Paul Morand in a quasi-fascist pamphlet 'France La Doulce', caricatured the French film world and called for a pogrom against those who were turning France into 'God's concentration camp'. It was indeed the reign of the commercial racketeer, speculators of any and every nationality, who took advantage of the easy opportunities to

70

exploit French film production after the collapse of the big firms. With only a few thousand francs for capital, such speculators created phantom companies, installing themselves in furnished offices, and buying a few pages of publicity in the industrial weeklies to advertise some new sensational production. In this way they sold films not yet begun, used the money obtained to get together stars and directors, and then started work. Usually such enterprises ended in bankruptcy before the film was completed. These practices were widely condemned; it was generally predicted that they would complete the ruin of the industry, and the French cinema was expected to suffer total extinction. Events after 1934, however, did not bear out this prophecy.

VIII

THE RENAISSANCE OF
THE FRENCH CINEMA—FEYDER,
RENOIR, DUVIVIER, CARNÉ

1934—1940

JACQUES FEYDER left the United States for good at the end of 1933. Only five years before he had set out with high hopes and great dreams of the immense technical and financial resources that would be his in Hollywood. All these he had indeed found, the generosity had been genuine, even to his being given the great Garbo for his first film. But he soon found that his personality was sterilized and his art reduced to nothing, as if by a Midas touch; he had never felt himself in sympathy with the huge American film factory, recently nick-named by von Stroheim 'the Sausage Machine'. During these five years Feyder had faithfully delivered tasty and well-seasoned dishes for international consumption, dishes which lacked body and vitamins (*Olympia*, *Le Spectre Vert*, etc.) As far as the development of his art was concerned they were completely wasted years. Back in France, after a few false starts and much talking, he was given the direction of *Le Grand Jeu*. With his wife, Françoise Rosay, his assistant, Marcel Carné and a whole troup of actors and technicians, he set out for a second time for North Africa, the country that had smiled on him during the making of his first success, *L'Atlantide*.

The script for his new film was by Charles Spaak. The advent of talking films brought with it a deeper understanding of the need for

72

genuine film subjects, with a result that screen-writers in France were becoming increasingly important. The French, with the exception of Delluc, had until this time sadly neglected the importance of a good script; it might even be assumed that the failure of the Impressionists to influence international taste was perhaps due, to some extent, to the absence among them of a leading script-writer, a French Carl Mayer.*

Charles Spaak, a prolific, skilful and cultured script-writer, was responsible for the scripts of some of the greatest successes of Feyder, Renoir and Duvivier; he also wrote some scripts that were quite mediocre. One of his chief rivals was Jacques Prévert, a poet of the Surrealistic school and really more of a dialogue-writer than a script-writer. He was responsible for the scripts of all but one of Marcel Carné's films; his approach to life and his bold style are easily discernible, so great was the impression he made.

Spaak and Feyder, working as a team, not only on this film but on all Feyder's European productions, turned this quite conventional story of the French Foreign Legion into an outstanding film. They gave the story a psychological background, taking the Pirandellian theme, so dear to the author of *L'Image*, 'can one ever be certain of the person with whom one is in love?' In order to emphasize even further the uncertainty of the poor hero, Marie Bell doubled the parts of the two women, but when the voices were recorded, a second voice was dubbed for the part of the prostitute.

The novel treatment of Marie Bell's dual role and the two voices was a success both for the film and for its influence on film history, but was no more essential to the success of *Le Grand Jeu* than was the clever trick photography in *Crainquebille*. If the film can be regarded as important, it is surely for its portrayal of the French Foreign Legion and its colonial atmosphere. The dominating characters were not Pierre Richard Wilm and Marie Bell, but Françoise Rosay and Charles Vanel as an ageing couple, the owners of a cabaret on the very edge of the desert. The nostalgic failure of human lives permeates the outstanding scenes, set in a stuffy backroom of the cabaret, where Françoise Rosay tells fortunes for homesick Legionaires. With Hollywood behind him,

*Carl Mayer will be remembered as the writer of *Caligari, Sylvester, Scherben, Der Letzte Mann, Berlin Symphonie eine grosse stadt*, and many other great German films between 1920 and 1930.

now once again out of his system, Feyder was able to give himself up to naturalism, the naturalism of Zola and Maupassant.

Pension Mimosas followed and surpassed *Le Grand Jeu*. Here Françoise Rosay was a modern Phèdre who is in love with her adopted son, and who, in order to get him away from her young rival, leads him to commit suicide. Spaak's script was more melodrama than tragedy; the real subject of the film was gambling, the Game of Chance: gambling at Monte Carlo, gambling in Paris society, gambling amongst the crooks and the would-be gangsters. The sets, by their very preciseness, took on an immense importance; the shabby boarding house, which gives the film its title, became one of the protagonists of the film, the gambling hall with the roulette table, so was the low night-club on the banks of the Seine where Françoise Rosay came upon her adopted son in the company of the would-be gangsters. From this film springs a new trend of French cinema, later to be developed by Marcel Carné.

Feyder's *Le Grand Jeu* and Duvivier's *La Bandera*, both with scripts by Spaak, are the roots from which sprang other new trends of French cinema. Duvivier had already made a score or so silent films, none of which were worthy of notice. They were mostly adaptations of Henri Bordeaux's novels—melodramas, adventures or religious propaganda. But talking films gave Duvivier a medium with which to pull himself out of the mediocre rut into which he had fallen. Starting with *David Golder*, in which Harry Baur gave a modern but very weak interpretation of Balzac's *Père Goriot*, Duvivier had a certain amount of success with *Poil de Carotte*. This film was remarkable for its fine photography, and the way in which Duvivier directed the young Robert Lynen, showing a fine understanding of the sensitivity of childhood. This latter quality is evident in an almost contemporary film by Jean Benoit Lévy— *Maternelle*, which might even be said to surpass *Poil de Carotte*. It painted a valuable picture, in the authentic French style, of the Paris suburbs, while Duvivier's film gently toned down the harsh and searching qualities of Jules Renard's story.

For the setting of *La Bandera*, Charles Spaak again used the background of *Le Grand Jeu* with one small difference—instead of the French Foreign Legion it became the Spanish Foreign Legion, commanded by General Franco, to whom the film was dedicated. There was very little space for a love interest in this film. However, it was in this that Jean Gabin was first noticed, playing the criminal seeking oblivion in the

74

Legion. The climax of the film was the rout of the Legionaires in a beseiged fort, an episode which recalled the recent success of *La Patrouille Perdu*, and a rough-house (showing that Duvivier was obviously influenced by the American gangster films) in which he used oblique camera shots for the first time. This technique he employed again later in some of the best sequences of *Carnet de Bal*.

La Bandera was a great commercial success. At about this time Jean Renoir finished his film *Toni*. This discreet, commercially unsuccessful and therefore, unfortunately, little known film marked the turning point in Renoir's life, and at the same time can be traced as the source from which springs the modern Italian school of Rossellini and de Sica.

For the background of this film, which he made for Marcel Pagnol, Renoir took a crime story from a newspaper, using his players as the witnesses of the crime. The story was really a focus on a current social phenomenon—a study of the conditions of Spanish and Italian emigrant workers in the farm-lands of the South of France. The excellent dialogue and apparently unrehearsed, natural acting of the players, coupled with the vivid photography, gave the film, twelve years before Rossellini, a stark realism of screen reportage. This work, strong and penetrating, opened up the path of true realism, and also took up arms for the emigrants and loudly proclaimed their cause.

The year 1934, a period of grave economic unrest in French politics, was the year that not only produced *L'Atalante*, *Le Grand Jeu*, *Dernier Milliardaire* and *Angèle* but also, in the Place de la Concorde, a riotous assault against the Palais-Bourbon. In the days which followed, popular counter-demonstrations replied to this show of strength; armed police were called out, and the dead were counted in dozens. Heralded by this grave tragedy, France entered a new pre-war phase. The evils of war, recently unleashed in Abyssinia and afterwards in Spain, showed the road that European history was soon to follow.

Enthusiastic movements sprang into being. Demonstrations became commonplace. Millions of men were joining together to prevent a rising similar to the one that had recently carried Hitler to power. The Popular Front burst into being with the enthusiasm of a new religion. That the French cinema was not slow to catch this new fire is seen in the *Crime de Monsieur Lange* by Prévert and *La Belle Equipe* by Duvivier and Spaak.

It has never been easy to appreciate fully the value of the excellent

75

dialogue in Jacques Prévert's *Le Crime de Monsieur Lange*, because the very defective recording made it almost unintelligible. This film had been made on a shoe-string by an independent producer. The reign of the money-conscious, yet gambling independent producers proved in the end to allow a far greater degree of freedom for the film directors than the straight-laced, penny-grabbing monopolies formerly imposed by the all-powerful big companies. By accepting work from these mushroom, and sometimes dishonest, production companies, directors and their colleagues ran the risk of not being paid for their efforts, and, what what was even more serious, of finding that the financial source was drying up or sometimes disappearing altogether before the end of their film was in sight. This indeed happened to Renoir during the making of *Nuit de Carrefour*. The film, as shown in the cinemas, made very little sense; this was not really surprising because half of the scenes were never shot. He was obliged to distribute the production in order to get back some money in return for the effort he and his colleagues had put into it. However, coupled with these hazards, was the glorious freedom in the choice of subjects and the method of treatment of the film. Any director at all who had any appeal with the public was assured a free hand by his undiscerning backer, while the rigid selection committee meetings of the big companies pitilessly eliminated any subjects that tended to deviate from the conventional. Out of the abject poverty of the French cinema was born its golden years, thanks entirely to this state of free competition.

Le Crime de Monsieur Lange was the story of a small printing firm in the Paris suburbs. The head of the firm, a crafty businessman, not unlike the shady new film producers themselves, withdrew from the bank all the firm's capital and disappeared. The employees, seeing no other way out, band themselves together and, with what money they are able to collect, undertake to print the popular novelettes of their neighbour, Monsieur Lange, who is excellently played by the star of *Le Million*, René Lefèvre. With the honest workmen in control of the business, the printing concern prospers. Hearing of this success, the unworthy proprietor tries to take over again. The indignant Monsieur Lange kills him.

When considered side by side with other films of this period, *Le Crime de Monsieur Lange* stands out like a sign-post. It was, however, neither intended to be, nor was it in fact a propaganda film. Prévert and

Renoir had, almost without effort, discovered the touchstone of popularity throughout France. They had learnt how to portray, in a style quite different from that of René Clair, the ordinary man in the street, the butcher, the baker, the humble clerk and the successful businessman, with the exactness that comes of deep observation, the exactness of Emile Zola and of Auguste Renoir, the father of Jean.

Renoir read the script of *La Belle Equipe* by Spaak just as he was finishing work on *Le Crime de Monsieur Lange*. He was full of enthusiasm to make the film, but Julien Duvivier had already obtained the rights and had set about making the film himself.

The story had a similar beginning to *Le Million*. A group of down-and-outs win a large prize in a sweepstake. But unlike Clair's impoverished gentle-folk of *Le Million*, who had no real material worries, *La Belle Equipe* were a group of unemployed, living in a wretched hotel. They are shown tramping the streets in a fruitless search for work, standing beside an advertisement that emphasized their misery, and, when they sit back in their miserable hotel room the proprietor cuts off the electric light as the hands of the clock point to nine. Then, in the unkind darkness of their rooms, their rage against the miserly landlord is just about to burst when they hear of their lucky win.

The prize, although considerable, is not enough to live on by itself. This story goes on where *Le Million* ended, showing the need of the community to work together if society is to prosper. The friends of *La Belle Equipe* work together for their mutual benefit by buying a broken down music hall and uniting their efforts to get it running again.

In certain respects, the film surpassed *Le Crime de Monsieur Lange* in showing that a little group of men of the right spirit, could, by working together, find the cure for the ills of modern society. *La Belle Equipe*, while still being the story of failure, yet managed to criticize, without pessimism, the fond French belief that to own a pretty white cottage with green shutters is the acme of happiness. Even so, the film ended ambiguously.

Nevertheless, whatever else the films of this period did, *Toni, Le Crime de Monsieur Lange* and *La Belle Equipe* established in the French cinema a new character, rarely to be seen in the films of other countries, that of the ordinary man in the street. This new character reached perfection in the Spaak-Duvivier film, with an outstanding performance by Jean Gabin, who succeeded, in his first effort, in putting over the man in the muffler. Under the muffler and the cloth cap were shown to exist human feelings of weakness and strength, tenderness, a quick understanding, courage, a temper easily aroused, a sense of humour and a strain of brutality. Gabin's success in this role brought him immediate international acclaim. His was a fine, sympathetic study of the French workman of the period.

As far as Jean Renoir was concerned *La Belle Equipe* was a frustrated desire and he now turned his efforts to an adaptation of Maxime Gorki's famous novel *Les Bas-Fonds*, in which he starred Jouvet and Jean Gabin, but without the success that such a team merited. His next film, however, *La Grande Illusion* undoubtedly re-established his reputation as a realist, already demonstrated in *Toni*; it was a great success. The subject of this film, whilst being less clearly defined than the story of *Toni*, was an unreserved attack on the burning question of war.

Little by little it was becoming apparent all over Europe that a world-wide upheaval could not much longer be averted. Thinking men and women did not like the only answer they could find to the question of how to meet the coming situation.

Renoir thought he had found an answer, a different one, and in *La Grande Illusion*, which he wrote with Charles Spaak, he set it down. He retold some of his own experiences as a young officer during many long years in German prisoner-of-war camps. The whole point of the film was to show that among individuals of similar temperament, there can exist a sympathy that transcends national sentiments, even though their nations may be at war one with the other. The prison is an old castle; against this background an aristocratic German officer and a young French officer, played by Eric von Stroheim and Pierre Fresnay, find a common respect and understanding on many subjects from the fundamental problems of life to their mutual enjoyment of a game of polo. In another part of the castle a common sympathy springs up among the private soldiers of both sides, offspring of similar social classes. Thus, *La Grande Illusion* shows that whilst war does not abolish social distinctions, it still cannot destroy human sympathies, which recognize no frontiers. Towards the end of the film the French prisoners hear of the victory of Verdun. To celebrate this they organize a musical entertainment, merely as an excuse for singing the 'Marseillaise' and annoying the Germans. The Germans in fact become furious. The Hun officer draws his revolver and shoots his 'friend', the French officer, when the latter is assisting an attempt at escape. Then, with genuine regret for his hasty deed, the German commandant subsequently places his last remaining flower on the French officer's coffin.

La Grande Illusion might be considered a last sincere, but already hopeless, appeal to the German people not to go to war again. It called upon the individual Germans to remember the spirit of international sympathy that existed at the end of the last war, and to disregard their war-mongering masters. To Dr. Goebbels the message in the film was clear. He not only forbade it to be shown in the Third Reich, but also persuaded Mussolini to ensure that it was not acclaimed at the Venice Film Festival.

Before collaborating on *La Grande Illusion*, Charles Spaak had written the script and assisted Jacques Feyder with *La Kermesse Héroïque*, a film which again dealt with the problems of war and offered yet another solution for them.

It may be said that the makers of this film did not fully appreciate how topical its story was to the Europe of 1935-40. After finishing his depressing *Pension Mimosas*, Feyder looked around for a gay story about the famous painters of his native Flanders. Charles Spaak had previously written a period novel set in Flanders which Feyder decided would be admirable for his purpose, that of telling the world of the great talents of his famous countrymen. Bernard Zimmer prepared the adaptation, and the cast included Françoise Rosay, Louis Jouvet and Alerme. The sets for the film were executed by Lazare Meerson shortly before he died. They consisted of a series of sumptuous scenes, like pictures, and gave a remarkable impression of a seventeenth-century Flemish village. This film showed that period films, properly handled, could be sure of a great future. Feyder possessed an exceptional sense of rhythm, and this important work had the ethereal beauty of a ballet. However, the story that he had lighted upon by chance was suddenly spotlighted by an unexpected parallel in the world politics of the day.

In the seventeenth century, the troops of the ferocious Spanish Governor of Flanders, the Duc d'Alba, were marching on a little town. The city fathers, hearing of the approaching armies, and knowing the dreadful massacre that would ensue, were terrified. The women of the town, sizing up the situation for themselves, decided to welcome the enemy. They hoped that by entertaining and feasting the soldiery they would be able to avoid bloodshed. The army arrived, and instead of

79

opposition they found a great banquet awaiting them—an heroic banquet. The next day the army moved on, leaving behind a townful of Flemish women, tenderly waving farewell to the men who had brought a flavour of adventure into the dull routine of their daily lives.

As *La Grande Illusion* had raised the question of the mutual understanding between nations, so *La Kermesse Héroïque*, as early as 1935, raised the question of collaboration. This film indicated that when national oppression is inevitable, organized resistance would be stupid; it suggested that the best way for the vanquished to safeguard their country from further wastage is to accept the enemy, give them such food as they require and a free run of the country.

However, if this moral was read into the film after 1940, it was certainly not in the minds of the producers when it was made in 1935. When it was first shown the only incidents that the film provoked were by the Flemish Nationalists, who were to be, paradoxically, a few years later, the worst collaborators with the Germans, while Feyder and his assistants on this film were persecuted by the Germans. In Berlin, under the patronage of Goebbels, the film was acclaimed as one of the most important of the year, and *La Grande Illusion* remained banned for the German public.

Renoir's next film, *La Marseillaise*, again had as its principal theme the topic of war. One of the best scenes showed the refugees at Coblenz plotting with the Germans, to attack Paris with the Duke of Brunswick's army. These, perhaps, original 'collaborators' put their own aims and desires above those of their country, and were ready to accept the Fatherland as masters of France.

Thus, *La Marseillaise*, while heralding a new war to the France of 1937, should have had as its culmination the battle of Valmy, where the victorious French soldiers made their historic charge, singing their newly acquired national anthem. Valmy was described by Goethe as the threshold of a new era. In actual fact, Renoir just glossed over this battle and portrayed the French soldiers being swallowed up in a fog, which is believed to be more historically correct than the version of the singing charge. The film was heavily criticized, often abusively; it was by no means an outstanding achievement, although it contained many fine sequences.

*   *   *   *

80

La Marseillaise had its premier in Paris six months before the Munich fiasco. . . . As soon as the first shock of the dark echoes had resounded through France, many people, including many film-makers, were overcome by fatalism, against which it seemed no human effort could prevail. Almost over-night, as can be seen in Pagnol's *Marius*, the French cinema switched to making films with a predominant, if subtle, theme of escapism.

When *Pépé le Moko*, directed by Julien Duvivier and scripted by the popular novelist and scandal-columnist Henri Jeanson, was released, it was credited with this new theme, greatly to the surprise of its makers. The film was much more than a French version of a Hollywood *Scarface* or *Underworld*. It was a very clever study of gangsterdom set in the colourful and infamous Kasbah of Algiers.

Jean Gabin, in the role of Pépé, was a character dreaming of escape. Pépé's escape was not into the Kasbah, that den of the underworld into which even the police did not dare to enter, relying instead on the integrity of their stool-pigeons. The Parisian comes to hate conditions in the Kasbah, especially when he finds that he is more securely a prisoner in his apparent 'escape' than if he had been locked up in the deepest of dungeons. He is homesick, and dreams of flight with the girl that he has met on a dream voyage—a treatment already expounded by Pagnol in *Marius*. The film ends at a symbolic and fatal iron gate which bars his way to liberty, and the girl of his dreams, now a real person, leaves safely on the slowly departing ship. The police catch him and coldly shoot him down . . . an ending that has since been repeated in Carol Reed's *Odd Man Out*.

Another film, very similar in theme but perhaps not quite so obvious as *Pépé le Moko*, was *Carnet de Bal*. Made as a shrewd commercial speculation with Duvivier as director, it consisted of a series of sketches designed to bring to the screen all the most successful and popular French stars of the day—Fernandel, Raimu, Harry Baur, Louis Jouvet, Pierre Blanchar and Françoise Rosay. A widow finds the dance-programme of her first ball some twenty years before. She decides to see if she can find any of her old friends, the men who had made her heart flutter on that night long ago. She finds them all, except one who has died, and they are all failures. Man is destined to failure, the hopes and aspirations of youth are but madness; all striving is in vain; only old age, degeneration and feebleness are certain. Significantly the best sequences

81

are those with Louis Jouvet and Pierre Blanchar, where the hero's decadence and failure are near complete.

The last film by Duvivier before the war in 1939 was *La Fin du Jour*, with a script once more by Charles Spaak. It told of the last sad efforts of a pitiful group of old actors and actresses, forgotten artists who tried to make a come-back in face of the insurmountable obstacles of physical infirmity and approaching death.

Spaak and Duvivier had travelled a long way since their early beginnings, Spaak with *La Grande Illusion* and Julien Duvivier with his *Golem*, which he made in Prague with its theme of revolt and the law of the slave.

Destiny, at the same time, had a controlling interest in the works of Marcel Carné and Jacques Prévert. The first film by this team of poet and ex-journalist was *Jenny*. With the trump card that Françoise Rosay had agreed to play the title role, Jacques Feyder had persuaded a small producer to back this undertaking by his little-known assistant of *Le Grand Jeu* and *Pension Mimosas*. In *Jenny* the great actress was offered the same type of role of an ailing mother that she had played so well in *Pension Mimosas*.

The plot was rather awkwardly melodramatic, but the beautiful closing shots with Françoise Rosay outlined against the sky on a small suburban railway bridge, showed that Carné, in a style particularly his own, was just as much a lyrical poet as the great masters of cinema, Jasset, Feuillade, René Clair and Jean Renoir, especially with the subject of the Paris suburbs.

For their next film they decided to enlarge on Prévert's first success, *L'Affaire Est Dans le Sac*. For this film, *Drôle de Drame*, England had to be shown in caricature, a pleasant friendly caricature with London in a haze of fantasy. However, Carné was not the man to pull off this humorous cocktail—he needed, like his master Jacques Feyder, to sense the real atmosphere of his story before he could, in turn, produce a real caricature. In *Drôle de Drame* the characters were people of the imagination who floated in front of impressionistic settings. This was a dip into the traditional French burlesque with a dash of Mack Sennett and 'l'Opéra de Quat'sous' rubbing shoulders with certain surrealistic theories. The result was heavy and cold where there should have been a fairy lightness of touch and a warmth of real understanding.

Following this near-success came *Quai des Brumes*, in every sense an outstanding film, and perhaps one of the most important of the pre-war period. The film and its title was taken from Pierre MacOrlan's book which told of the famous cabaret Le Lapin Agile in the Montmartre of 1914 and of its distinguished clientèle, Picasso, Francis Carco, Apollinaire and Max Jacob. Jacques Prévert, while retaining MacOrlan's atmosphere and background characters, lifted the cabaret bodily to a dock-side backstreet in Havre and into the pre-war period of 1939. A deserter, Jean Gabin, arrives at the port looking for a ship in which to escape from the police; he has committed a murder during a fit of temper. While still searching for a likely ship he falls in love with Michèle Morgan and her nostalgic beauty. They both want to get away and start a fresh life together in a new and distant land. Their way is barred by her despicable guardian (played by Michel Simon) and his gang of disreputable cronies. Gabin manages to kill the guardian but is seized by the leader of the gang, played by Pierre Brasseur. For a second time he is involved in murder, and his unhappy fate prevents his escape to a new life.

When they entered the film world, both Prévert and Carné held in very high esteem the work of Murnau and von Sternberg. They were convinced that the gangster was the true hero of this period, and such films as *Underworld* seemed to them right because they showed the machine-gun defying the world, the only way of overcoming social injustices.

By 1930, however, they had altered their ideas, and the gangster-superman appeared to have far too much in common with Hitler's SS men; so the gang leader in *Quai des Brumes* was not shown as a hero but as a coward.

The rebellious Jean Gabin was not a professional gangster, but an unfortunate, pushed into murder by petty social injustices. Murder for him was not a way out, but an added misfortune. All he asked of life was to be allowed to live in peace, far from the noise of civilization, with the woman he loved. But as in the old fairy-tales where the forces of good and evil used to fight at the foot of the cradle for the soul of the infant, so here these forces were fighting around the bed of the unhappy lovers; the evil forces are represented by the girl's guardian, a shop-keeper and retailer of illicit goods, and the gang of ruffians; the forces of good are the tramp, the painter and the general public. In these fairy-tales evil always wins. Happiness is not to be found in this world; the good people

83

and the lovers are destined always to be defeated and kept apart; the battle of life has as its goal the satisfaction that comes from doing kindly actions—but in the end there is nothing but the certainty of defeat.

To a certain extent it may be said the *Quai des Brumes* followed up and developed some of the points raised in von Sternberg's *The Docks of New York*. Carné's next film *Hotel du Nord*, was the development of an idea expressed in Eugene Dabit's outstanding novel on the lives of ordinary men and women. The story is rather similar, in some passages at least, to Rouben Mamoulian's *City Streets*, especially where the hero and the heroine as poor, abandoned, destitute lovers find themselves faced with no alternative but suicide. This film lacked the smoothness and the unity of *Quai des Brumes*—perhaps because Prévert had no hand in it. For all the rare intensity of the poetry in many of the shots, such as some of the views of Paris and, especially, the canal of Saint Martin, the film belongs to the group of Carné's minor works.

Out of the dark shadow of the approaching war, Carné emerged with his masterpiece, the *Le Jour se Lève*. It resembled von Sternberg's *Underworld* in that the hero, hounded by the police, kills himself at the end. Gabin in *Pépé le Moko* was safe, provided he stayed in the Kasbah where he had plenty of friends and lovers. Gabin in *Le Jour se Lève* is hopelessly alone, in a shabby top-floor room with the hours numbered against him and ticking away. In the ultimate depth of despair, he forces himself to live his last few hours before the final, inevitable annihilation.

The success of this super-dramatic situation was only achieved by Carné and Prévert as the result of long hours of great effort and intense deliberation. Their hero was a simple foundry worker, in love with a little flower-shop assistant. His chance stumbling on to the road to crime and death was brought about by a broken-down circus dog-trainer (Jules Berry) and his mistress (Arletty). The skilful characterization of this pair is pure cinema. The absolute degradation of the dog-trainer is superbly defined more by the back-ground against which he is cast and his actual bearing, than by the dialogue. He *is* corruption; he *is* vice and complete evil. The flower girl (Jacqueline Laurent) is essentially feminine, indefinite, ingenious and perverse. The worker, in his undervest and cloth cap, speaks with the pseudo-intellectual clichés of St. Germain-des-Prés, and chooses his metaphors with a view to emphasizing the drama of humanity and the utter inescapability of destiny.

84

Le Jour se Lève, offspring of crisis, turmoil, and much soul-searching, was a perfect example of artistic achievement. Jean Gabin reached the peak of his art in a role that might have been written for him. Arletty, bitter, sly and debased, yet whose heart is fundamentally kindly, is partnered by a despicable, weak, ignoble Jules Berry, sneakingly listening at keyholes, seducing young girls, torturing his team of dogs and reeling off lies as easily as he breathes. He personifies all the evils of human nature and ironically his fatalistic outlook gives him the added strength with which to live his dreadful life.

At a time when the world stood on the threshold of a new war, the French cinema seemed to have been injected with a fatalistic despondency. Carné was sunk in a quasi-metaphysical confusion. He was a strange mixture of the bitterness which characterized his master, Feyder, bitterness which was not natural but rather developed by experience; at the same time he had a profound sympathy for his fellow-men and a sensitive appreciation of human frailty. In this last respect he differed greatly from Duvivier, to whom man seemed fundamentally and hopelessly bad.

*   *   *

Meanwhile, Feyder was on the move again. *La Kermesse Héroïque* behind him, he went to London and directed for Alexander Korda *A Knight Without Armour*, with Marlene Dietrich and Robert Donat. This turned out to be, for him, as great an error as his Hollywood incident, but it did not, of course, last so long. About this time he made in Munich a French and German version of *Les Gens du Voyage*, which was an interesting film. The scenes in it of the giant travelling circus are excellent, but the complications of a melodramatic and childishly stupid plot completely eliminated the effect of Feyder's usual outstanding qualities, his fine direction of actors, the conviction with which he builds up atmosphere, the clarity of his story and the sharpness and yet fluidity of his photography. It is a great pity that he, who had been the most enthusiastic crusader for the golden age of the French cinema, should not only have chosen this time to waste his efforts on facile camera reproductions, but also that he should choose this particular moment to be away from France. The last great film he made in France, *La Loi du Nord*, was not seen until the German occupation had been in force some while, and then only after it had been completely mutilated by subsequent 'editors'. It suffered greatly from being staged in an America reconstructed in French studios: some exteriors were, however, shot in Norway, in the then completely unknown port of Narvik. Its tragic anticlimax occurs when all three heroes, who passionately love the same woman, meet their ultimate deaths through her.

The strain of the immediate pre-war era is also evident in Jean Renoir's film of this period. Gone was the happy optimism of *Le Crime de Monsieur Lange*, leaving in its place just bitterness and despair. *La Bête Humaine* was taken from one of Zola's most unhappy and mediocre novels. In spite of Renoir's obviously sincere effort to give a faithful reproduction of his inspiration, the stories of film and book are quite transformed. In Zola, the mechanic Lantier was the victim of the fate that was haunting the Rougen Macopiart family.

Renoir is expressing his own mood, or perhaps a mood of the times, when he indicates with some bitterness that it is only a whim of human nature that prompts the first step, however stumbling, on the road to crime. Carné, as if in agreement, had already shown his Gabin falling almost accidentally into crime.

If this film had been made at the same time as Feyder made *Thérèse Raquin*, there is no doubt but that the emphasis would have fallen on the heroine whose insatiable, sensual thirst fed her hatred of men and prompted her to crime. However, *La Bête Humaine* coming as it did in this era, Renoir throws the spotlight on the man doing his job of work. The passionate interlude is there, but dictated by Renoir's mood at the time, it takes a secondary place. As a documentary the film is doubly valuable—the two journeys from Paris to Havre shot from the footplate of the engine are superbly edited, and the film contains a graphic portrayal of the daily life of an express-train driver.

Ever since *La Chienne*, Renoir had been fascinated by ideas for the use of deep focus photography to emphasize the action of the film. He turned aside from conventional methods, using photography and different depths of focus to fuse characters into their surroundings as the temper of the plot required. At times he arranged that the background was as clear and sharply defined and as much in focus as the foregrounds. It was not surprising that at the time he was adversely criticized for such revolutionary ideas, but three years later Gregg Toland introduced these theories to the United States. Renoir was fully aware of the many uses that could be made by varying the focus of the lens. Sjöström had already used the technique of fading the background completely out of focus in *Les Proscrits*, when he wanted to spotlight the action into the centre of the screen without any distracting background. In the murder scene of *La Bête Humaine* (which is basically the same as the one in *La Chienne*) the man and woman stand out against an almost non-existent background, and in both films the impressive blending of a song is used to isolate the central characters from the rest of the world.

Renoir's last French film was also one of his finest. For this comedy, staged in the luxurious surroundings of a wealthy property, Renoir omitted all the usual props and dramatic sequences. The story was already well known, the novelist, Paul Bourget, having published it as long ago as the end of the nineteenth century under the title of *Cosmopolis*. The core of the film concerned a great reception which ended in tragedy. Other films, *Les Bas-Fonds*, *La Grande Illusion*, *La Bête Humaine* had all been made around similar themes.

Besides writing the script and the dialogue, Renoir also took one of the principal parts. By careful planning he arranged that much of the film was made in its proper sequence, scene by scene—quite an exception to the normal routine of film making. *La Règle du Jeu* was made under, perhaps, the most favourable of conditions, its director was in the prime of his life, master of himself and of his art, and yet it was a complete failure. The film was withdrawn from general distribution only a few days after its first showing, and was never again offered to the open market. A few weeks later the war broke out, and the film was banned by the censor, and so ended its short career both in France and elsewhere.

This film has, however, outstanding value because it is the only French work that covers the period from the days of Munich to the early months of the war. It may be said that Jean Renoir did achieve the ambition recorded in the epitaph to his works: that at a similar epoch he should give to France a work of equal magnitude as *Le Mariage de Figaro* which Beaumarchais presented on the eve of the Revolution.

It was unfortunate that Renoir misjudged completely the public taste of the moment. The greyness of international events demanded a gay dramatic relief in entertainment. In spite of himself, Renoir had become involved in a conflict of expressions. At the end of the film, when a series of slapstick blunders result in the tragic death of the most sympathetic of heroes, the moods of the film were so much at variance that the sequence, which was intended to be emotional, became only ridiculous. Renoir, blinded to all else by his new-found enthusiasm for amateur acting, at times completely abandoned direction of the film, with the inevitable result that many of the characters lacked conviction, and discrepancies crept into the story.

The climax of *La Règle du Jeu* was, as in *Le Million*, a glorious filmic chase. The luxurious reception rooms of the castle offered an ideal background for the antics of the jealous gamekeeper, who, firing a revolver in all directions, tries to stop his wife, the parlour-maid, from being pursued by the local poacher. In another part of the house some guests, in the costume of Bavarian peasants, are rehearsing on an improvised stage the famous soldier's song 'En revenant de la Revue', a song which since the early days of Méliès' youth, had been used as the signature tune of the reactionary followers of General Boulanger. The owner of this valuable estate, a renowned collector of mechanical gadgets, is proudly exhibiting his musical instruments to a group of visitors. The lilt of their primitive music spurs on the gamekeeper and the band of domestics in their three-cornered love-chase, while a fight develops between the family and all their guests over the charming hostess; the chase begins, regardless of all obstacles that block its path. The scene gives way to a macabre dance by ghosts and skeletons. This brilliant sequence, following the chase, is an ideal cinematic metaphor, drawing with rare imaginative foresight a parallel to the disturbed and varied emotions of 1939. Renoir was busy shooting these very scenes while Hitler's entry into Prague was being announced over the loudspeakers of the world. This lovely corner of France, the Salogne, with its castles, its forests and marshlands, a country famous for its hunting, whose natural beauty and tempo Renoir had so successfully captured, was but one year later to see the last sad battles of the French troops in the terrible year, 1940. Historically speaking, *La Règle du Jeu* was both in style and in theme absolutely the film of the moment.

Renoir had built up great hopes for this film and when he found that it was a failure he lost confidence in himself. He went off to Rome and plunged his energies in to a 'safe' subject; he directed the film of the opera *La Tosca*. About this time, 1939, René Clair came back to Paris to direct *Air Pur*, a film with children as the principal players, and became very aware of the influence of the approaching war on the film industry.

88

Mobilization had already commenced and the growing uncertainty completely disorganized the Paris studios. For several years France had been producing 125 films a year, but in 1939 she only completed seventy-five.

If, by their talent, Renoir, Feyder, Marcel Carné and René Clair had dominated the French cinema during the years 1930 to 1940, they were by no means the only film-makers of that period. Exponents of the old silent films were kept very busy with the new medium, but of all their works nothing worth remembering remains.

Abel Gance, after finishing *Napoléon*, made a pompous film, which was a complete failure, it was distributed as a talkie under the title of *Fin du Monde*. After this he seemed condemned to make, as director or as producer, mediocre films like *Le Roman d'un Jeune Pauvre*, *Lucrèce Borgia*, *Jérôme Perrau* or *Le Maître de Forges*, with an occasional re-make of one of his former triumphs, such as *Mater Dolorosa* and *J'Accuse*. Perhaps his best film was *Un Grand Amour de Beethoven*, containing some interesting experiments in sound technique but unfortunately spoilt by Harry Baur's over-acting. His very moving *Paradis Perdu* had considerable charm.

Marcel L'Herbier made a considerable number of films; he seemed to specialize in historical reconstructions like *Le Mystère de la Chambre Jaune*, *Le Bonheur*, *Le Scandale*, *Les Hommes Nouveaux*, *La Porte du Ciel*, *Veille d'Armes*, *La Citadelle du Silence*, *Forfaiture*, *Nuits de Feu*, *La Tragédie Impériale*, *Adrienne le Couvreur* and *Entente Cordiale*. Baroncelli continued his practice of filming successful plays and adaptations from popular novels like *L'Ami Fritz*, *L'Arlésienne*, *Le Père Goriot* and his very successful series set in the French colonies with *S.O.S. Sahara* and *L'Homme du Niger*, as well as an occasional patriotic melodrama, which invariably missed the mark and ended as a grotesque piece of clowning, like *Nitchevo* and *Feu*. Leon Poirier's films were on similar lines (*Soeurs d'Armes*, *Brazza*, *L'Appel du Silence*) all of which had a documentary quality indicating that he spent a considerable amount of time in experiments of this kind. A talking version of *Les Misèrables*, in several parts, brought considerable laurels to Raymond Bernard, but some of his other films are best forgotten, *Anne Marie*, *Coupable*, *Cavalcade d'Amour* and even *Otages* which, although it had an intriguing subject, was spoilt by a weak script.

The record of those who joined the industry after 1930 and seemed at the time to offer new hope for the French Cinema, was no more successful. Of them all, Marc Allegret was the most brilliant. His *Lac Aux Dames* was a great success, a success that he tried to repeat with *Les Beaux Jours*. When he tried yet a third similar film, *Sous les Yeux d'Occident*, it almost seemed that he no longer had the strength for such achievements, in spite of the fact that this film brought to the screen Jean-Louis Barrault. *Gribouille*, with a good script by Marcel Achard, was very well acted by Raimu; and Bernstein's *Orage*, with Charles Boyer, revealed the very attractive talent of Michèle Morgan, who, with Jean Gabin, had perhaps the most famous and typical profiles in the pre-war French cinema. *Entrée des Artistes*, although intelligently made, lacked conviction; its interesting search for documentary atmosphere in the Paris Conservatoire was spoilt by a melodramatic script by Henri Jeanson.

Pierre Chenal, after his very dreary *Mutinés de l'Elseneur*, which completely ignored public taste, went in for melodrama with *l'Alibi* and *La Maison du Maltais*. His later films *l'Affaire Lafarge*, the story of a famous law-case, and *Le Dernier Tournant* from James Cain's novel, *The Postman Always Rings Twice*, were a little better.

Jean Benoit-Lévy found real success with the charming, sensitive *Maternelle*, and then made a string of failures, *Itto*, *Hélène* (adapted from Vicki Baum) and *Altitude 3,200*. His *Mort du Cygne*, though somewhat over-dramatic, again showed promise and was a good documentary of the Ballet. Dimitri Kirsanoff, after the failure of *Rapt* which was none the less interesting, seemed content to accept box-office certainties, but he managed to inject them, from time to time, with some of his own interesting experiments—*Franco de Port*, *La Plus Belle Fille du Monde*, *L'Avion de Minuit*. *Quartier Sans Soleil*, a story of life in the slums, although sympathetic, was clumsy and melodramatic. Claude Autant-Lara, after directing *Ciboulette*, an operetta, assisted by the young novice, Jacques Prévert, made several films for Maurice Lehmann, all of which were below average: like *Le Ruisseau* and *Fric-Frac*. The latter, adapted from the successful play by Edouard Bourdet, was very well acted by Michel Simon and Arletty.

Foreign directors, living in France, were responsible for very few productions at this time. Léonide Moguy, a Russian, started with a stirring music-hall film, *Le Mioche*, and worked his way to the polished *Prison Sans Barreaux*, in which two new actresses made their first appearance, Corinne Luchaire and Ginette Leclerc. It was a clever production: all the more astonishing when followed by *Conflit*, *Je t' Attendrai* and *L'Empreinte du Dieu*, all carefully made but completely lacking in fire and imagination.

G. W. Pabst, after *Don Quixote*, a fine photographic album but completely devoid of feeling, and his failure in Hollywood, produced only decadent efforts such as *Le Drame de Shanghai*, *de Haut en Bas*, *Jeunes Filles en Détresse* and *Mademoiselle Docteur*, in which the only relic from his early *Threepenny Opera* is his taste for setting his stories in low and disreputable surroundings. Anatole Litvak, after a remake of Maurice Tourneur's silent film *L'Equipage*, found considerable financial success with *Mayerling*, which took its director and stars, Charles Boyer and Danièlle Darrieux, straight to Hollywood. This successful film brought no artistic advancement to the French cinema, neither did Kurt Bernardt's gay operetta *Le Vagabond Bien Aimé*, Max Ophül's sensitive but dull *Werther*, Robert Siodmak's *Mister Flow*, a remarkable pastiche of Lubitsch's famous *Trouble in Paradise*; *Ultimatum* the last sad film of Robert Wiene, director of *Caligari*, so shortly to die; Fédor Ozep's pompous *Dame de Pique*, Farkas's quite ordinary *Bataille* or Tourjansky's *Le Mensonge de Nina Petrovna*.

French critics were amazed that the films of Sacha Guitry's plays should be so successful in countries outside France. When this author-actor first appeared in the cinema, early in the twentieth century, he was chiefly noted for his original ideas. But later, in the between- war period, his comedies were so stereotyped and repetitious that they had no individual charm or freshness. A few of these were filmed (*Le Mot de Cambrone*, *Désiré*, *Quadrille*), but what was surprising was the audacity with which he carried out the idea of making a film, a whole evening's entertainment, with himself continually in front of the cameras. This he did by exploiting the medium to the utmost, and by using many varied make-ups. Working along these lines he made his cleverest film, *Le Roman d'un Tricheur*; this was almost a silent film in technique, but it had a running commentary. A mere trick and, by a happy fluke, it worked this once. On the other hand, *Les Perles de la Couronne* and *Remontons les Champs-Elysées*, which was a series of pompous vulgar sketches, were no better than third rate music-hall.

Sacha Guitry lived the life of a man-about-town. Pagnol, a colleague of his from the theatre, was far more conscious of his surroundings, and relied on the feel of the earth and the scent of the country for his very existence. This actor-producer, who had already had a success with *Angèle*, was busy trying to make another success of *Regain*, adapted from a novel by Giono. It was the story of an abandoned village in Haute-Provence with a 'back-to-the-land' theme as a cure for war, for unemployment, and, in fact, for all the evils of humanity in the machine-age. This idealistic film, spoilt to certain extent though it was by one or two mistakes, might have been a much greater film if it had actually achieved what it set out to do, which was to portray the simple life of the Provençal villages.

Marcel Pagnol was on surer ground when he was making *La Femme du Boulanger*, also adapted from a story by Giono. It was just a simple tale, a farce written in the style of a lesser Molière. The baker's wife in a little village elopes with a handsome shepherd, and the heartbroken baker refuses to bake his bread. After much persuasion he agrees to go back to work, while the whole breadless village unites and assists in the search for the missing wife. She is found, and once more everything is in order again. Raimu's natural talent and Ginette Leclerc's sensuality, together with the convincing simplicity with which the local characters of this Provençal village, the priest, the schoolmaster, the mayor, the squire, are painted, make the *Femme du Boulanger* one of Pagnol's finest works. Indeed, it takes second place only to *Angèle*. In spite of its close theatrical associations, this film is a good example of the French school of the day, and it is easy to understand why it was such a great success outside France, in London, and to an even greater degree in New York. This amusing and, in some respects, powerful work should not, however, be allowed to overshadow the large number of other more original and more powerful films that were at this time coming out of the French studios.

If the high hopes that accompanied the advent of the 'talkies' had not yet been fully realized (not even by Georges Lacombe, whose *Les Musiciens du Ciel* was genuinely remarkable), the immediate pre-war years were still to produce some important personalities.

First among these was Jean Grémillon. The unhappy failure of *La Petite Lise* closed the doors of the French studios to him. For a short while he worked in Spain (making *La Dolorosa*), and then made several French films in Berlin. The first of these were not more than average, but *Gueule d'Amour*, beautifully written by Charles Spaak from a novel by André Beucler set in Toulon harbour, showed virile qualities, later

92

to be evidenced in *L'Etrange Monsieur Victor*, in which Raimu had one of his best parts. *Remorques*, following *Gueule d'Amour*, had many beautiful scenes such as the sad wedding in the sea-side pleasure garden, so brutally interrupted by the grim news of a ship in distress . . . everyone deserting the celebrations to go to the rescue. Although the subject was slightly strained, Jacques Prévert's treatment and dialogue gave it a certain conviction, and, in addition, there was everywhere ample evidence of Grémillon's gift for characterization.

Jacques Prévert was also one of the team responsible for the successful and exciting *Les Disparus de Saint Agyl*, adapted from the detective novel by Pierre Véry. The story was set in a boy's school just prior to 1914. The director, Christian Jaque, already the maker of several successful commercial films, now followed in the path of Duvivier. He was deeply interested in this new medium, and became so engrossed in it that he finally reached near perfection. The script was by Jacques Prévert, although his name is not given in the credits. He fired it with such a poetry and understanding that the film became alive and real, and when Christian Jaque later came to direct *L'Enfer des Anges*, he was surprised to find these qualities missing from the later film. These successes, however, won Jaque a deserved recognition, and his output ceased to be a series of mass-produced melodramas. Another pre-war film that achieved distinction was Jef Musso's *Le Puritain*, an expressionist version of a novel by Liam O'Flaherty, with Jean-Louis Barrault and Viviane Romance.

Almost on the eve of the Second World War, the novelist André Malraux showed, only once in Paris, the film he made in Spain during the last months of the Civil War. It was called *Espoir*, and was the adaptation of a few scenes from a book of the same name. Made after the style of the silent Soviet cinema, it had in some episodes a flavour of the gangster film. Many causes delayed the finishing of the film, and then the war delayed its full distribution. It was put away until 1945. It is thought to have influenced Italian neo-realism, but being locked away for so many years, it cannot have been seen by many, although it does have much in common with the late Italian school. In certain of the crowd scenes, the author, carried away by Spanish influence, is supremely successful, but the other sequences, where his characters dwell on the conditions of human suffering, have a false ring, and are poorly played by indifferent actors. When shown in France after the war, the public, coming straight from the battles of liberation, quickly felt its insincerity and artificiality, and received it coldly. The film was an attempt by an author at filming literature, and in much it was unique, although it had little influence on the French school.

In 1939, in spite of *La Règle du Jeu* and *Le Jour se Lève*, the new French school seemed to be showing marked signs of weariness. And just when it looked doubtful whether the cinema would find its renaissance, the dreaded and inevitable war broke out.

IX

THE FRENCH FILM DURING THE OCCUPATION

IN September, 1939, war was declared, completely interrupting French film activity. Nearly all players, directors and technicians went into the Services; the majority of the studios were requisitioned by the military authorities and were converted into barracks or depots. Amongst films in production at the time which were never finished, was *Air Pur* (Fresh Air), the film about children which René Clair was directing in Paris. This film is a sad loss to the cinema.

The new war was known at first as the 'phoney' war, since it lacked action. Like a game of football or cards, films were useful to amuse idle troops. Extension of leave was granted to certain technicians and actors, and production revived a little. Among the few films made at the time, the most notable was Julien Duvivier's *Un Tel Père et Fils*. It was produced in Paris by an American company, from a script by Marcel Achard and Charles Spaak. This sort of *Cavalcade* with many of the best-known French players such as Raimu, Michèle Morgan and Louis Jouvet was extravagantly made, and related the story of a French family from 1870 to 1940. It was very reminiscent of *Carnet de Bal*, not so much because of its episodic treatment, but because almost all its heroes suffered defeat. The editing of this official propaganda film was hardly finished before the German entry, when Julien Duvivier left Paris. At Bordeaux he embarked for Hollywood, taking with him a copy of the film, which was afterwards shown in Allied countries under the new title of *La France Immortelle*. A short epilogue, made in America, showed Michèle Morgan in Occupied Paris. This last sequence, unfortunately, was hardly a logical conclusion to a series of episodes featuring

95

such characters as an elderly roué and a drunken colonial. This mediocre film, typical of a certain pre-war trend, emphasized even more the latent defeatism characterizing official propaganda, then directed by the subtle author of *La Guerre de Troie N'Aura Pas Lieu*, Jean Giraudoux.

Then the real war began on the Western Front. When Paris was occupied, Dr. Goebbels controlled all films in a France governed by Marshal Pétain. Productions henceforth had to submit to two censorships, the German one of the *Propagandastaffel* and that of Vichy, under presidency of the writer Paul Morand, which had effect only in what was called the 'free' zone. These two bodies censored not only the finished films, but the scripts even before production began. No work could be started, therefore, without their consent.

Important German capital was invested in the industry. For ten years preceding the war, German productions, either openly or camouflaged, had—after American films—jostled their way into first place for playing time on French screens; in July, 1939, about 30 per cent of foreign films shown in Paris were of German origin. As soon as Paris was occupied, Dr. Goebbels made haste to consolidate and extend this stranglehold exercised by his companies *Ufa* and *Tobis*, and temporarily set aside during the period of the 'phoney' war. He became involved in all branches of the industry, printing laboratories, studios, the cinema press, production, distribution and, lastly, cinema circuits which led to his acquisition of numerous 'key theatres' belonging to non-Aryans. About one-third of the entire French film industry thus became German property. In Paris, Dr. Goebbel's own production company, the Continental, was spending huge sums of money.

German and a few rare Italian films were the only new foreign productions shown on French screens. In the so-called 'free zone', however, the exhibition of British and American films was authorized until the beginning of 1942. The monopoly of French playing-time by German pictures met with certain obstacles. Even though Paris, still dazed by the defeat, whistled snatches of tunes from *Bel Ami*, Willy Forst's dull, insignificant Viennese operetta, Nazi films quickly discouraged the French public. Yet Dr. Goebbels had produced the cream of his best and most ambitious films to win over Parisian audiences, productions for which he had been responsible since appropriating the German industry for himself. Very few of the frankly propaganda films reached Paris, these being kept as a treat for Hitler's 'supermen'.

The majority of German films shown in France were insipid comedies or vague historical reconstructions, music-hall shows or detective stories. In common with Hollywood, German production found inspiration in newsreels. Occasionally, it was all too evident as in *Jew Suss* and *Ohm Kruger*. Even in minute doses, propaganda was keenly resented by the sensitive French, who spontaneously boycotted German programmes. The proportion of box-office receipts earned by French-produced films had been estimated at about 60 per cent or 70 per cent before 1938; as a result of this unwise German appropriation of programme space and the consequent boycott by audiences, the proportion went up to 85 per cent during the Occupation. This increase in receipts explains the relative and very paradoxical prosperity of the French industry during a period when all export was forbidden.

Two hundred and twenty films were made in France during the four years of Occupation. Almost without exception, French directors and film writers managed to avoid the pit-falls of collaboration, and the majority were even able to 'resist' actively. Their clandestine organization Le Comité de Libération du Cinéma Français headed by Pierre Blanchar, Jean Grémillon, Louis Daquin, Jean Painlevé, Jacques Becker and others, helped to play a decisive part.

*　　*　　*

From the beginning, the Occupation posed fundamental questions to film-makers regarding the conception and direction of their work. Consciously or not, they almost all realized that it was impossible to continue pre-war themes under such conditions. To teach, for example, that man should submit to fatalism was degrading at a time when resistance to the horrible fate hanging over their country was of prime importance. Other subjects had to be found.

Jean Renoir and René Clair had joined Julien Duvivier in Hollywood, where they found the characteristic, pre-war ideal couple, Jean Gabin and Michèle Morgan. To escape from the Gestapo, Jacques Feyder and his wife, Françoise Rosay, took refuge in Switzerland. Almost alone, Marcel Carné stayed in Paris. At the beginning of the Occupation his first production plan was symptomatically entitled *Les Evades de l'An 4000*. All sought escape from the unsavoury present in dreaming of other times, past or future.

97

Dr. Goebbels's Continental company did nothing to discourage this tendency. Since Hitler schemed to make Paris the Luna Park of National-Socialist Europe, it was considered advisable for France to specialize in films of comic or dramatic entertainment, planned to replace Hollywood productions on the screen.

The first Continental pictures were *Premier Rendez-Vous* directed by Henri Decoin, and was a perfect substitute for the American light comedies, and *Le Dernier des Six* a Parisian detective thriller, directed with a certain skill by Georges Lacombe from a script by H. G. Clouzot. But the Continental was not always free from the taint of propaganda, even in detective stories. Thus the screen-writer Clouzot had to adapt a pre-war novel by Georges Simenon, *Les Inconnus dans la Maison* to show how a young 'non-Aryan' could divert the good, provincial women of the *bourgeoisie* away from their rightful path. In the finale, Raimu, as a barrister, in his summing-up quoted favourite catch-phrases of the Vichy Press.

Les Inconnus dans la Maison appeared to continue the criticism of manners, a characteristic of pre-war French films, but for the sake of appeasing Dr. Goebbels, the result was to stigmatize French 'corrup-tion'. Many of those who did not want to embark on such a course, shared the feelings expressed by the former Minister of Propaganda during the 'phoney' war, Jean Giraudoux. A novelist-dramatist of re-finement, he had stated during the early years of the Occupation, on agreeing to provide typically sensitive dialogue for what promised to be a showy and vulgar film version of Balzac's novel *La Duchesse de Langeais*, 'Our era no longer asks a man of letters for works. . . . It claims, above all, a language from him. What is expected now is not that the writer speaks the truth, like the jester to a complacent king, but that he should reveal it to himself, entrust himself with it, so as to allow it to organize his thought and feeling, the secret of which a writer, alone, is the trustee.'* During the Occupation, the majority of French directors, prevented by the *Propagandastaffel* from telling the truth, went to the opposite extreme and became absorbed in brilliant fantasy—a direct contrast to the search for reality practised by the pre-war school. Great Parisian film successes during the Occupation were *La Nuit Fantastique*, *Les Visiteurs du Soir* and *L'Eternel Retour*.

Marcel l'Herbier, the director of *La Nuit Fantastique*, from a script

*Quoted by Roger Régent in "Cinéma de France" (Paris, 1948).

by René Chavance, had wanted to call his picture *Le Tombeau de Georges Méliès*, as tribute not to the maker of *L'Affaire Dreyfus* or *La Civilisation à Travers les Ages*, but to the conjurer of the Robert Houdin Theatre, and the 'trick' inventor of the charming *Voyage dans la Lune*. With this film, the best that he had directed for twenty years, Marcel l'Herbier brought to life some of his youthful dreams, those of the old impressionist school. He added his own gifts of good photography, technical prowess and careful work, while his script-writer Chavance introduced all the obsolete bric-à-brac of a kind of surrealism.

Les Visiteurs du Soir was welcomed with enthusiasm by a large public. Failing to escape as far forward as the year 4000, Marcel Carné went back to the Middle Ages, to the times of the Devil and his spells. The script by Pierre Laroche and Jacques Prévert takes the audience into a huge white castle in the fifteenth century. A great feast is being held and the devil sends his disciples to mingle with the jugglers. These scenes have real beauty, and reveal Carné's great plastic gifts at their best. Costumiers, actors and musicians make up a team, steeped in medieval French traditions, which bring ancient miniatures to life with perfect taste and technical skill. In contrast to Laurence Olivier's *Henry V*, the transposition was skilful enough never to appear like a tracing from the original document.

After this brilliant start, interest waned. This exercise in style seemed like something frozen. The world of Carné and Prévert was almost unchanged, although in medieval disguise; on the one hand are the Good beings, those sanctified by love (in this case the couple are the troubador and the young mistress of the manor, played by Maria Déa and Alain Cuny), on the other hand are the Evil ones, led by the Devil himself— Jules Berry—who became identical here with Destiny as in *Le Jour se Lève*, where he played a similar part. In the minds of the script-writers, the Devil was to be a portrait of Adolf Hitler. But in the finished film, this allusion was not realized, with the exception, perhaps, of the last scene. The Devil petrified the young couple beside the fountain in which are mirrored the warlike tournaments which brought the triumph of Evil. In spite of the Devil's anger and the torture they have endured, the lovers are reunited. Beneath the stone of the joint statue in which they are imprisoned, their hearts beat in unison one, two, three ... it was an image of captive France herself. And for the first time in the work of Carné and Prévert, Destiny and Evil were powerless to conquer Love and Goodness.

Les Visiteurs du Soir enjoyed an extraordinary success. Soon afterwards, *L'Eternel Retour*, directed by Jean Delannoy, also followed this new fashion.

Jean Delannoy, whose career is rather similar to that of Julien Duvivier, had before the war been a purely commercial director, prolific and mediocre. His latest film on the eve of hostilities was a fairly good melodrama in Hollywood style, *Macao ou l'Enfer du Jeu*. During the Occupation he suddenly attracted attention with his film *Pontcarral*. Although it did not entirely escape complacency, tediousness or a certain vulgarity, it did show proof of a real flair for production. But in 1942, it was a film of special significance, an illumination in very vivid colours, delighting the public by its subject matter. In creating this historical film, set in the reign of Louis XVIII, the script-writer Bernard Zimmer had maliciously underlined everything that the Restoration of 1820 had in common with Vichy. These allusions escaped the censor, but were unfailingly applauded by hilarious audiences who did not miss a single parallel. The hero, a colonel of the Empire who, with his home as barricade, fought off the enemy, became a symbol of the Occupation period. A few months later, one of the military heads of the French Resistance called himself Pontcarral as a nickname, so widespread then was the double meaning of this film.

L'Eternel Retour, when shown in London after 1945, was thought by some British critics to be typical of the collaborationist film. Jean Marais plays the lead, that of a big, blonde Aryan, in a subject dear to Richard Wagner. It is either little known, or forgotten, that in France the old Breton legend of Tristan and Iseult is less well-known from the opera than from the famous version written by the troubadors, Béroul and Thomas, and popularized in modern French by Charles Bédier. To the French public, this illustrious theme is a cultural treasure, with no taint of collaborationist tendencies; in addition, the patriotism of the beloved director of *Pontcarral* was never in doubt. As for Cocteau, essentially a poet, the modernization of an 'eternal theme' had for a long time been a favourite obsession of the author of 'Oedipe', 'Chevaliers de la Table Ronde' and 'Roméo et Juliette'.

Although *L'Eternel Retour* can refute accusations of collaboration, it can hardly be defended in any other respects. This fine old legend, freely disfigured by the script-writer, is weakened more by the ponderous additions of odd and unwarranted episodes than it is by its transposition

100

into a vaguely contemporary epoch. The great love, which is the dominating theme of the original story, is not retained in spite of a few good shots of the 'ideal' couple, Madeleine Sologne and Jean Marais. On the other hand, the hideousness of the lecherous dwarf, evil and grimacing, and the extraordinary vulgarity of some of the details are unduly oppressive. When the two lovers were dying in the final scenes, the muffled sound of a motor-boat was reminiscent of the hearts beating under stone in *Les Visiteurs du Soir*, where the fantasy was more skilfully used.

Another script by Cocteau for *Le Baron Fantôme* recalled German expressionism. This film was received with almost total indifference. But escape was to be found elsewhere than in mere repetitious fantasy. The happy, pre-war eras of 1914, or even of 1870, and the charm of past times inspired Claude Autant-Lara and his script-writers, Pierre Bost and Jean Aurenche, to find a form of expression. Autant-Lara belonged to the *avant-garde*, but with the possible exception of the operetta *Ciboulette*, he had never chanced upon a film which could give true scope to his personality and desire for freedom of expression. In the *Mariage de Chiffon*, *Lettres d'Amour*, and especially in *Douce*, he proved himself an excellent director of players; in his sets he showed a very marked artistic taste fostered in earlier days when he had been set-and costume-designer for Marcel l'Herbier. *Douce*, the best film he made during the Occupation, showed some bitterness and a certain power beneath the rather sugary display of charms and trimmings which had enfeebled his two preceding films. Odette Joyeux played the remarkable, perverse ingénue, supported by Marguerite Moreno and Roger Pigault. The conclusion was reminiscent of that of Jean Renoir's *La Règle du Jeu*, the pungent social criticism there being reduced to a faint disapproval of manners in *Douce*, the moral becoming merely conformist, and so weakening the whole work.

Robert Bresson's *Les Anges du Péché* was set in present times, away from the world inside a convent. This detachment allowed a discussion of the 'eternal' spiritual problems in the very midst of the Occupation. Jean Giraudoux's dialogue, the most accomplished he ever wrote for the screen, was, according to his own aim, a perfect exercise in style rather than a work of art. The direction of Robert Bresson, an ex-art photographer, achieved a symphony in white with brilliant facets, a sort of crystal scaffolding with sharp, clear-cut angles.

This work—and *Les Dames du Bois de Boulogne* which followed it—

101

can best be described as 'abstract', a term often used for the *avant-garde*. Bresson, sensitive to plastic qualities, had a taste for almost metaphysical universality and an intellectual, rather than formal, severity, all of which led him to the verge of abstraction. *Les Anges du Péché* was saved from the realm of the absolute by the character of the heroine, a nun devoured with pride and self-assertion beneath her cloak of outward submission and humility. In the narrow world of the cloister, dramatic tension arose from battle originating in pinprick annoyances and a rivalry between the women.

In Robert Bresson's second film made during the Occupation and shown the day after the Liberation, dramatic tension was lacking. *Les Dames du Bois de Boulogne*, originally entitled *Les Dames de Port Royal*, was in fact dominated by a slavish devotion to Jansenist severity, akin to that of Jean Racine. The subject, belonging to the eighteenth century, was an adaptation set in present times of one of the episodes from Diderot's 'Jacques Le Fataliste'. A haughty marchioness, jilted by her noble lover, took her revenge by introducing a loose girl to him as a well-born woman, and succeeding in goading him into such an infatuation that he marries her. In the Bresson—Jean Cocteau version, the chief characters were a worldly woman, a businessman and a cabaret dancer, but they were systematically extracted from their social environments and placed like duellists in a Racinian drama away from the world in a noble and bare setting. To make this drama believable, the mainspring must function perfectly, but such a misalliance is no longer scandalous as it was in the eighteenth century and to-day lacks any impact. A mistake in the casting of two important parts added to the overall mistake of the film's conception. There remained the harsh, evil character, played by Maria Casarès, a spider weaving a mortal and crystalline web, and Bresson's own qualities, the cold and brilliant symphony of his photography, his ability, though often clumsy in detail, for formal perfection.

The 'stylistic' tendency of the Occupation was crowned by a masterpiece, *Les Enfants du Paradis*, the richest and most perfect film by Carné and Prévert, a true treatise on style. Needless to say, the author's favourite theme was there again: the impossibility of happiness and great love in a badly designed world. Lasting three hours, the film had the breath and breadth of a great novel. Prévert's characters were not all of one piece—they developed with time. Evil was incarnated in the person of a very wealthy Balzacian nobleman (Louis Salou); Good was the warmhearted mimer Debureau (Jean-Louis Barrault), absorbed in creating a great art for the people, a forerunner for the authors of the 'true screen masters, those who speak to the whole crowd' (Louis Delluc).

The dividing line between Good and Evil in *Les Enfants du Paradis* was less rigid than usual. Lacenaire (Marcel Herrand), a romantic Lacfadio, was a very intellectual criminal; both an anarchist and a murderer, he was to his creators more sympathetic than antipathetic. The devoted wife (Maria Casarès) hid beaneath her outward gentle virtues, the unswerving ferocity of a religious fanatic. And the courtesan (Arletty) in her splendour and her misery could love, but could also sacrifice love to money. In the closing shots, the hero on the trail of the woman he loves is engulfed and lost in the happy carnival crowds. This last scene is reminiscent of the ending in King Vidor's *The Crowd*, but here its meaning, although ambiguous, was different; the hero was not in opposition to the mass. He was drowned, or rather he melted into it, becoming a man amongst other men, whereas in *Les Visiteurs du Soir* the chief characters were placed on a pedestal which detached them from their environment. The incidental characters remained even more indistinct by reason of Carné's photographic technique, their flow of movement always merging into the background.

This magnificent and sumptuous film, this gigantic, philosophical ballet was essentially an aesthetic soliloquy on the relations between art and life, the comparison of different forms of art to each other. The chief styles of the romantic period—the fair-ground show, the melodrama, the comic parody, the dramatic mime and the Shakespearean tragedy, each appeared in turn, and each was descriptive of the dramatic content of the film. From the aesthetic angle, the ending might also be interpreted as the fusion of man in a kind of universal spectacle, in which creator and public blended into the same human comedy. The comparison, in the background, between the cinema and the theatre, the silent film and the talking film, gave a more intense interest to all these forms of the art of spectacle. But this very subtle and very apt aesthetic finesse meant less to the public than the splendours of romanticism in a Paris coming from Balzac and Eugène Sue, the sumptuous pretexts used by Prévert and Carné to develop their multiple metaphors.

Les Enfants du Paradis was the accomplishment of perfection for the

French cinema; much more than a step forward, it was an end rather than a beginning. Yet the pre-war works of Carné and Prévert were still having repercussions in studios throughout the world, while *Les Enfants du Paradis* exercised no special influence. This film, even more than *La Kermesse Héroïque*, remained a splendid, isolated monument.

French directors were not solely occupied with the search for style during this period. In spite of the fact that the necessities of Occupation forced a change-over, the pre-war realistic tendency, of which Jean Renoir had been the leader, still found an outlet.

One of its followers, Jacques Becker, had become a director during the war, after having been Jean Renoir's assistant for ten years. His first film, *Le Dernier Atout*, a brilliantly worked-out but fundamentally simple detective story, was meant as a substitute for American films, now cut off from the public. The commercial success of his film gave Jacques Becker a certain standing.

Goupi Mains Rouges, an adaptation of the novel by Pierre Very, was planned as the typical, conventional detective drama. But the complications of the plot became in the end a pretext for fantastic and poetical flights of fancy. The descriptions of the lives of different types of peasant living in the centre of France were very exact, minute, almost finicky, but they were very well done. *It Happened in the Inn*, as the picture was called in America, is a better title than the French one, because the inn is really the pivot around which most of the movement revolves. Worthy of special mention is the admirable playing by Fernand Ledoux as the peasant poacher, reserved and thoughtful.

In *Falbalas*, shown after the Liberation although completed before, Becker attempted a description of the daily life of a huge Parisian fashion house. The almost vulgar banality of the plot was again an excuse. The failure of the attempted flights of poetical surrealism hid, for many critics, the real, deep qualities of the work. In contrast to the work of Carné, in these two films by Becker the background and even the foreground are more important than the characters themselves, with all their dramatic intrigues. The preparation and presentation of a composite theme, the life of an upper middle-class family during the Occupation, were the chief centre of interest in this uneven piece of work. In this film the director asserted his own style, and emerged as strongly differentiated from his master, Jean Renoir. Becker proved himself subtle, yet firm, but more spontaneous than powerful. He prefers minute description, often tinged with irony, to critical, satirical analysis. Becker may be better compared to a Dégas analysing, with sharp, meticulous eye, the exterior of the corridors in the Opera or the laundresses' work-room, rather than to the popular fullness of a Renoir senior melting into the crowd atmosphere at the Moulin de la Galette; a gay tenderness in Becker, the director, replaces the sharp, almost cruel, dissection so dear to Dégas, the painter.

Louis Daquin's *Nous les Gosses* had the special merit of being one of the first films of the Occupation period which did not hide its leaning towards reality. The script had been originally written before the war, and there was very little added to it to recall, even indirectly, the period of Occupation. A group of children in a poor Parisian quarter join together to make amends by collecting money to pay for a wilful prank. The film's value lies mainly in its honesty, its integrity and its robustness. Social inequality is emphasized, exhorting the need for comradeship among the poorest classes. *Nous les Gosses* fully deserved its wide success. After this promising start, great things were hoped for from Daquin. He then undertook, with commendable vigour which did not, however, help the finished result, a mountaineering film *Premier de Cordée* which failed mainly owing to its questionable script. Louis Daquin had then to wait until after the war to make a come-back.

Jean Grémillon, with whom Daquin had worked as assistant, was the greatest representative of the realistic tendency and reached his peak during the war. *Lumière d'Eté*, scripted by Prévert and Laroche, showed Good and Evil once more in conflict, with the former as a dam in construction peopled by engineers and workmen. Evil was the local castle with its guests; a degenerate, criminal aristocrat, his mistress (an ex-dancer now the proprietress of the small mountain hotel) and a broken-down painter, drunken and apathetic. Between the two, the heroine chose Good, whilst the workers on the dam rallied themselves into pushing the loose-living lord into an abyss. The conclusion reached was very different from Prévert's pre-war stories; Evil destiny no longer had the upper-hand, and Good triumphed in the company of the majority of men. Admirably photographed by Louis Page, the best parts of the picture were scenes showing a fancy-dress ball during which a frenzied farandola crowns the oaths and curses of a drunken Hamlet (Pierre Brasseur), the troubled secrets of a sadistic criminal (Paul Bernard), and an abetting complacent lover (Madeleine Renaud). The ending is

H

especially fine where, after the fancy-dress ball, in a setting showing the mountain and the dam on a morning of capital execution, the evil characters wander, dressed up as literary personages, which are the keys to their own characters (a caricature of William Tell, a lamentable Hamlet, a dubious Manon Lescaut, a new embodiment of the Marquis de Sade), but it is spoiled by an overload of melodramatic elements. The film's chief weakness lay in the characters on the dam, who are modelled only as it were, in bas-relief. The castle and its occupants, on the other hand, were described in such clear colours that they were obviously intended to symbolise the corruption then upheld by Vichy.

Le Ciel est à Vous again revolved around Good, this time in an even more striking form. The extreme dignity of this important work often made its real meaning a little obscure to those who saw it after the Liberation, when much of the impact, given to it by conditions peculiar to the Occupation, ceased to exist. Louis Page's photography, contrary to that of *Lumière d'Eté* is here extremely bare, as uncontrived as a newsreel. Similarly, the script, in many respects, suffers from banality. In a small provincial town, a garage-owner and his wife (Charles Vanel and Madeleine Renaud) share a passion for flying, and end up by winning a world record. In reality, two ordinary Frenchmen, who had actually achieved this, inspired the script-writers, Charles Spaak and Albert Valentin.

The director transformed this subject into the usual allegory. These working people, ready to sacrifice all they hold dearest—their piano, business, parents, even their children and their own lives—in order to attain their ideal, were, on the eve of Liberation, meant to represent those average French people, who are often considered faint-hearted, living safely on their own modest incomes, yet who in the end risked everything, even their lives, to support the armed resistance inside their country. Soon they were going to be seen in Paris, sacrificing their cherished Henri II sideboards to the barricades. This realistic portrayal of a little-known form of French heroism rang out, like a call to arms, for those who understood the message.

In the clandestine Press, the whole-hearted success of *Le Ciel est à Vous* was a contrast to the unpopularity, on moral grounds, of the last big film produced by Dr. Goebbels's Continental, *Le Corbeau*.

René Chavance's script, written sometime before the war, had been inspired by a then famous news item in France, the anonymous letters

106

of Tulle. G. H. Clouzot, a specialist in detective films, saw in this script a very well-designed thriller. The Crow, the mysterious author of the anonymous letters, terrorizes a little town, and better even than in the most classical of detective plots, each character without exception can be genuinely suspected. To the absorbing interest of this involved story was added an exceptional skill in the direction of the film. Clouzot proved his admirable knowledge of his craft, and of his film classics; in some episodes the influence of other masters of screen technique was almost too evident.

Le Corbeau, with its deep pessimism, also followed pre-war trends. In Carné, or even Duvivier, if evil fate always had the upper hand, there did exist also men of good will. Chavance and Clouzot tried to show that there is evil sleeping in the heart of every individual, and therefore humanity is to be wholly condemned. In one of the major scenes (where the influence of German expressionism is clearly evident) a swinging lamp throws the players' faces alternately into light and then into shade—from Good to Evil.

Since the film was obviously set in the French provinces, the Continental thought of using it for anti-French propaganda, and showed *Le Corbeau* in various European countries. French prestige was still high and, unfortunately for Dr. Goebbels, the results of this distribution fell very far short of his hopes. The Swiss, the Czechs and everyone else, rejoiced to see a good French film whose artistic quality was so far superior to the decadent mediocrity of Hitler's productions.

After the Liberation, the military censorship banned *Le Corbeau*, and those responsible for it, the script-writer and producer were evicted from the industry. These sanctions, which only lasted a short while, became the pretext for a campaign which idealized the martyred film as the summit of French art. This was, however, far from being a tribute to remarkable genius. In fact, Clouzot, at a later date, suffered more from this overpraise than from the temporary suppression of his film.

*   *   *

Towards the end of 1945, Allied bombardments and, in particular, the action of the Maquis, gradually paralysed transport and electricity. Finally, all cinematographic activity had to cease. In Paris, theatres were only open during the daytime, and cinemas were completely closed.

The Liberation found the film industry in a complete state of disorganization and decay. During the fighting period, the most striking film produced was the one made by technicians mobilized by the Comité de Libération du Cinéma. It was all made on the actual barricades used during the freeing of Paris. This unique, gripping newsreel had a great international success. Meanwhile, production was starting again, but under much difficulty, and shooting could only take place during the rare hours when unheated studios could be supplied with electricity. Productions made during the last winter of the war are recognizable by the clouds emerging from the players' breath, unless the director had remembered to take the precaution of making them suck ice before each shot. Raw stock was no more plentiful than electricity, but everyone alike was experiencing these same temporary difficulties, and it was with courage and hope that the French cinema, proud of not having betrayed its country at any time during the Occupation, entered the post-war phase.

X

AFTER THE WAR

1945—1950

THE last five years in the history of the French cinema are too near for us to be able to judge them with sufficient detachment. At best we can only generalize about a few of the more outstanding trends in its development. Its economical history is perhaps easier to describe, being based immediately on fact.

By the end of 1946, production had almost reached its normal pre-war output. In that year, ninety-six films were completed in comparison with an average of 120 before the war. French studios were too few in number. They were in bad condition and ill-equipped, and they functioned like the ships in the favourite legend, that claimed battleships in France are made in the kitchen with old bits of string! However, the high quality of the skill shown by the technicians made up in large part for the material defects.

Immediately after the war, equipment was estimated to be insufficient for production to recover its pre-war level. In France, as in other countries, the length of time needed for making a film had substantially increased since 1935. The Press, therefore, urged the Government to finance the construction of a French Hollywood on the Côte d'Azur to accommodate producers unable to find studio space elsewhere.

Eighteen months later the Press had to campaign again, but this time for the opposite reason; Parisian studios were obliged to close their doors, one after the other, because of lack of work. In January 1948, film-players and technicians banded together to draw the public's attention to the industry's serious situation. In certain branches of film-making unemployment reached the level of 75 per cent of the manpower.

It was estimated that this quick reversal in the situation was mainly due to the commercial agreements signed in May 1946, in Washington by the former Président du Conseil, Léon Blum, and the American Minister for Foreign Affairs, Mr. Byrnes. The Blum-Byrnes Agreement annulled the quota fixed before the war, which limited the number of dubbed American films introduced on the French market to 120, a figure equivalent to that of French production itself. By these agreements a screen 'quota' was adopted. The term was also used in the British Cinematograph Act, but there it was given a very different meaning.

The British quota, admirably progressive, has generally been fixed above the industry's capacities. The Blum-Byrnes quota was retrogressive and fixed far below the actual possibilities of home production. The treaty, in fact, established a figure of 37 per cent of the programme time, while the proportion for French films had, before the war, been as high as 60 per cent and 70 per cent, a proportion largely exceeded during the Occupation. Apart from this quota, no limitation was now imposed on the introduction of dubbed films into France, which immediately flooded the home market by the hundred.

In the first quarter of 1946, the French share in the producer's fraction of the box-office receipts fell to 39 per cent, while the American rose to 51 per cent. It will be remembered that in 1937, the French share had been between 60 per cent and 70 per cent, Hollywood's 25 per cent. During the war it had generally mounted above 80 per cent.

With these new conditions imposed by the Blum-Byrnes agreements, panic seized the production branch of the industry. In France, the producer's financial position is restricted, since a very limited national market cannot leave him a big margin of profit; furthermore, for language reasons, export is also limited. Outside a few specialized cinemas in New York and London, the great English-speaking public scarcely knows Parisian productions. This explains why (according to the magazine 'L'Ecran Français') a Scottish student, a few years ago, asked his teacher why France had never produced a film! Apart from these key markets, France has maintained steady outlets in Central Europe, the Scandinavian countries, the Near East and Latin-America. But this latter transatlantic market is threatened by Hollywood, and other competitors, especially since French exports are frequently disorganized, third-grade films too often gaining priority over works of quality. Lastly it must be remembered that the French-speaking public is limited beyond French national frontiers to certain parts of Belgium, Switzerland and Canada—in all, only a total of 60,000,000 individuals, a much lower figure than the English, Russian and even the Arabic-speaking populations.

France has 5,000 cinemas, and this figure is approximately equal to that for the whole of the British Isles. But in a country which is still largely agricultural, the majority of its cinemas are very small, and open no more than three days a week. Finally, the prices of seats are not high. In 1949 the average price of admission was 50 francs (1s.). This scale could hardly be raised because of the low average in the financial standard of life for the majority of the French population. In 1948, increases in admission prices were accompanied by a decrease in attendance of more than 10 per cent over the whole of the country; in the poorer localities this drop reached 25 per cent to 30 per cent.

The effect of this position in both the external and internal markets was an exceptionally low return from the exhibition of French films. The average cost of production, in 1949, was below 45,000,000 francs, a figure showing a large increase on previous years. In 1946, Marcel Carné's budget for *Les Portes de la Nuit* was considered an incredible folly, jeopardizing French production. Yet this budget hardly came to 80,000,000 francs (£100,000 sterling), which seems ridiculously low in comparison with the costs of *Caesar and Cleopatra* or *Joan of Arc*.

The crisis in French production can be understood when it is realized how the Blum-Byrnes agreements deprived it of an important share in the resources to be derived from the national market. The threat hanging over an art which had excelled from its very beginning soon moved the public. Throughout the whole of France, Committees for the Defence of the French Film were formed, and succeeded in stirring up Parliament. At the end of 1948 the Blum-Byrnes agreements were revoked, and the quota rate raised. The quota of 120 American films was re-established, and a surtax was charged in the cinemas. This was put into a fund to help the French film and by 1950 this fund had amounted to 2,000,000 francs. Although very insufficient, both these measures did provide the industry with some stimulation.

Production, which had fallen as low as 74 films in 1947 (as against 94 in 1946 and 120 before the war) reached 96 in 1948. But quality was very far from keeping pace with this relative increase in quantity. The slenderness of the budgets drove the most highly qualified film technicians away from the studios.

A striking characteristic of the post-war French cinema was that its chief men of talent had almost all abandoned production. During the five years since the Liberation (1944-49), René Clair, Claude Autant-Lara, Jacques Becker, Jean Grémillon, Julien Duvivier and Marcel Carné had each been able to direct and present one film only in France. Jean Renoir did not return from Hollywood. Robert Bresson had not been able to set his foot in a studio, and Jacques Feyder, returning from Switzerland, died in 1948 without having been able to direct a single film in four years.

French production, relying on its technical superiority, had to budget its very limited financial resources very carefully and frequently used unknown and inexperienced directors in preference to those who were internationally-known; the more commercially successful such directors were, the more it was feared that their fees would be too heavy.

In spite of these material conditions, far worse than those of 1935, the French post-war film is succeeding in maintaining its artistic level. But this re-awakening in the new post-war conditions presents many problems, some of which are not yet solved. Marcel Carné's *Les Portes de la Nuit*, a disappointing half-failure, was significant proof of this.

*　　　*　　　*

After the international triumph of *Les Enfants du Paradis* the prestige of Carné and his script-writer, Jacques Prévert, was so high that they were allowed the fullest possible scope in the choice of subjects. Their next film was an amplification of a ballet subject, written a long time previously by Jacques Prévert, which turned with acute observation to contemporary reality. Opening with a panorama of the Boulevard de la Chapelle, Paris, it bore the following comment, 'Paris during the hard winter following the Liberation'. The opening shots of *Les Portes de la Nuit* reconstructed the atmosphere to perfection, although there was no exterior shooting and everything had to be done on studio sets, which had been carefully studied down to the minutest detail. The staircases at the Barbes Rochechouart tube station during the rush hour were impeccably reproduced, complete with the very same crowds of working people rushing to and fro—a collaborator far more at ease than his son,

112

a member of the pro-German 'Milice', a black-market restaurant where officers, dug out from the depths of wardrobes and redolent of moth-balls, rubbed shoulders with businessmen foraging in the wake of the Allied armies—were all drawn true to life. The public recognized these familiar scenes from such well-known contemporary life. Without doubt, this description of Paris excelled in genuine realism even the realism of such films as Rossellini's *Paisa* and de Sica's *Sciuscia*.

The total commercial failure and partial artistic failure of *Les Portes de la Nuit* was due to such scenes as that when the child, the messenger of Fate, which is personified in the film by a vagabond called Destin, led the hero into a demolition contractor's workshop, where he found the 'woman of his life', the 'great love' which he had been seeking since adolescence, and the hero, until then only sketchily drawn, began to discourse on the Leeward Islands, the South Seas, Departure, the Beyond, Escape and so on. There entered into this film of 1945 a man from 1925, an ancestor of Pagnol's *Marius*. He started to preach that travel alone was capable of allowing 'dangerous living', and his dialogue, in a Paris which had so recently been bristling with barricades, seemed more than a little out of proportion. There had been no need then to look far away in order to flee from the 'monotony of daily life'; all too stirring adventure was on the front-door step.

In the American burlesque picture *Hellzapoppin*, a red-skin lands in the midst of a love-scene and apologizes; he has been mistaken and got into the wrong film! In *Les Portes de la Nuit* the hero mistook the entire film, as well as the post-war atmosphere. Out-dated themes, formerly borrowed from the lives of Gauguin and Rimbaud, no longer corres-ponded to the feelings of the new public. Because this truth had not been understood, *Les Portes de la Nuit* was a failure. If Carné and Prévert had known how to depict the last winter of the war in striking visual terms, they proved themselves incapable of discovering that it had a new poetry.

Although, taken altogether, *Les Portes de la Nuit* was a lamentable failure, it did not put the finishing touch to pre-war subjects. The Carné-Prévert team rested on the laurels of previous commercial successes. In post-war France, economic necessity made producers search for stories far beyond the usual recognized literary successes, theatre repertoire or best-selling novels. The directors were then ex-pected to repeat such box-office winners as *Pépé le Moko* or *Quai des*

Brumes. It was forgotten that the success of these pre-war pictures had been as much due to their novelty as to their deep sympathy with the thought of the times, but all that had been some years ago. These commercialized revivals of rehashed subjects resulted in mechanical copies of ancient formulae. The French pre-war film had been a reflection, good or bad, of contemporary reality, but the post-war imitations went on repeating endlessly such faults as they had had, usually in the form of a convention for aping a 'naturalism' far removed from actual life.

Dedée d'Anvers and *Une si Jolie Petite Plage* are both typical of this naturalistic tendency. Directed by Yves Allegret, the plots are handled, unquestionably, with great skill. Allegret is a director who knows all the resources of brilliant editing and photography. For these pictures he had, in addition, such fine players as Gérard Philippe, Bernard Blier and Simone Signoret, one of the most gifted actresses of the post-war phase. In France these films did have a limited commercial success, as some audiences still enjoyed the taste of the dead past. In the International Festival at Venice, *Dedée d'Anvers*, bringing nothing new, went unnoticed. The scripts of these films were almost parodies of *Quai des Brumes* and *Pépé le Moko*, and even surpassed them in their atmosphere of despair. Almost the entire action of *Dedée d'Anvers* takes place in a brothel, and everything centres around ignoble characters, fit only for extermination. In the final shot, at least, some hope does appear with the gleam from the lights of the workmen as they cycle off to work. As a second-hand murderer, who, knowingly, refuses escape for suicide, the hero of *Une si Jolie Petite Plage* (Gérard Philippe), brother to the Gabin of *Le Jour se Lève*, is resigned to his fate beforehand.

The naturalist tendency, particularly characteristic of Yves Allegret, was followed by Julien Duvivier's *Panique* and *Au Royaume des Cieux*. No less characteristic was Blistene's *Macadam*, which had some artistic quality, through being supervised by Jacques Feyder.

G. H. Clouzot's post-war films are similar in theme to the old pre-war naturalistic tendency. This gifted director achieved his peak with *Quai des Orfèvres*. The subject, an insignificant detective novel, was of neither interest nor importance, and devoid of any deep meaning. In short, the director repeated the old Hollywood formula of restimulating the banal subject-matter of a moderately well-planned plot by adding a picturesque study of some social circle. Clouzot had a perfect under-

114

standing of how to portray the actual Quai des Orfèvres (the French equivalent of Scotland Yard) and the most up-to-date Parisian café concerts, and to these portrayals he brought all the good taste, plastic feeling and artistic culture usually lacking in corresponding American productions. Certain scenes recalled the art of Manet, Dégas or Lautrec. The value of the film, as a whole, lay entirely in its form and in the quality of its photography. The insignificance of the actual story pushed considerations of morals and manners into the background; it is almost an apology for the ambitions of a young singer with no scruples, who trades solely on her pretty face.

After this mediocre plot, Clouzot was asked to undertake a subject worthy of his great talents. He pleased everyone with his choice of *Manon*, and he took the famous novel written in the eighteenth century by the Abbé Prevost intending to change it into a pitiless picture of youth torn by the chaos of immediate post-war times. *Manon* roused the greatest anticipation and on its opening day the public fought to get in to see it until the police intervened. This initial eagerness made its subsequent failure all the more marked.

Clouzot overcame the somewhat conventional, pre-war pessimism by aiming, in particular, at effect. In *Quai des Brumes* the pure love of the Gabin-Michèle Morgan couple combated against Evil, personified by the 'gang' who triumphed in the end. Manon was nothing more than a prostitute, who cared only for money and made her lover, Des Grieux, share this mania. Their love was defined by one of the key speeches in the film's dialogue: 'Nothing is disgusting when one is in love.' Manon says this when he knows that she had just sold herself to some old man. Her infatuated lover follows her throughout her criminal career. Love is represented in *Manon* with masochistic and perverse resignation, and Evil is represented as inevitable and almost desirable.

The film also suffered from weakness in direction, which, unlike Clouzot's other films, was marred by overloading, bad taste, and unevenness in handling the lapse of time; the French Liberation, the Parisian black market and the Jewish-Arab war in Palestine, were false and superficial in treatment, inspired more obviously by news items from the lurid press than by any true sense of reality. The picture was characterized by a self-conscious striving after big effects and sensation. It taught French films, at least, how to avoid the particular pitfall of theoretical abstraction. The failure of *Manon* revealed the one thing

115

necessary for the French school to win back its old fame. It needed to probe deep beneath the surface and find a fresh approach to the entirely special post-war conditions.

A fresh approach was not easy to find. The majority of the best post-war films succeeded only in being superficially accomplished. They failed to show any careful research. Claude Autant-Lara, in his best film, *Le Diable au Corps*, adapted from Raymond Radiguet's early novel, which was set in the last months of the First World War, tells of the desperate love affair of an adolescent boy and a slightly older discontented married woman. The screen-writers, Pierre Bost and Jean Aurenche, achieved a remarkable adaptation, and the acting of the two stars, Micheline Presle and Gérard Philippe, was outstanding. The young hero, thoroughly disorganized by the war, saw no other way out than through a kind of moral suicide, an all-embracing despair. A new 'mal-du-siècle' had taken hold of certain young intellectuals of Radiguet's generation in 1920. But conditions were different for the corresponding generation of 1945. The climax of the Resistance brought out the best in it, but on the other hand the Black Market had defiled the adolescent. Complete isolation had become an exception rather than a rule, even for a limited group. The *mal de la jeunesse* had become collective rather than individualist.

These circumstances lessened, in part, the effectiveness of *Le Diable au Corps*. Claude Autant-Lara had undoubtedly proved his mastery in the artistic sphere. Owing to the position in the French studios, he had to wait until 1950 before he could start work on a new film, but then he was given a subject which he would have chosen spontaneously. *Occupe-toi d'Amélie* was an intelligent and distinguished adaptation from a vaudeville burlesque of 1900 by Feydeau, a sort of *Italian Straw Hat* which, although technically perfect, lacked the observation and humanity characteristic of Labiche. Autant-Lara was thus thrust back on to the 'obsolete' and escapist type of film-making which he had specialized in during the peculiar conditions of the Occupation period.

Le Silence est d'Or (1947) was the first film finished by René Clair in France for fifteen years. It had tenderness, seriousness, melancholy, and clearly aimed at depth, which had not always been the most striking characteristic of Clair's work at the time of *Le Million*. Having reached maturity, the director soliloquized on old age in a subject for which he had found inspiration in Molière's *L'Ecole des Femmes*. A too-communi-

116

cative, elderly man (Maurice Chevalier) unwittingly teaches his younger rival (François Perier) how to win the woman they both love. The title *Le Silence est d'Or* not only came from the proverb but was also an allusion to the time when Pathé and Méliès had discovered the gold mine of the silent cinema. Out of respect for his childhood memories and the masters of his early youth, René Clair set his action in Paris in 1906, describing the period with tender irony. It was his best film since his departure from France. If we prefer *Le Million* or *Le Chapeau de Paille*, it is probably due to their novelty to present-day audiences. But it is not certain that posterity will maintain the same favourable judgment. Nowadays, the public admire *Le Voyage au Pôle*, made by Méliès when he was middle-aged, more than the films of his youth, which, although they were then new, are now thought less perfect. René Clair did not create a movement with *Le Silence est d'Or*; neither had he succeeded in doing so previously. Perhaps the optimistic irony of his conclusions stood in the way. And even he too, had to wait until 1950 to complete his next film, *La Beauté du Diable*, in Italy.

Jean Cocteau's *Les Parents Terribles* crowned the author's film career. It was an adaptation of the play which had marked the summit of his dramatic career in 1936. This technically remarkable experiment in filming theatre showed a family of the lower middle-classes, suffocating in a flat littered with the curiosities of bad taste. Pre-war 1940 (the date of the play's success) was joined to pre-war 1914 by a plot which, almost too well-handled, was close to the boulevard plays of the beginning of the century. Cocteau, poet, essayist, novelist, playwright, scenario-writer, painter and journalist, is an individual festering in a hot-house encumbered with poetical odds and ends, and locked to the outside world. In this respect, his film was, to a certain degree, autobiographical. Prior to this picture Cocteau had been maintaining the tendencies he had formed during the Occupation. His *La Belle et la Bête* was, in truth, a ballet, luxurious and accomplished, but superficial. Cocteau's two other works, *Ruy Blas* and *L'Aigle a Deux Têtes* which followed the same trend, were frankly mediocre. Up to a point, pre-war feeling also persisted in *La Symphonie Pastorale*, filmed by Jean Delannoy from André Gide's most famous novel with an academically flawless technique. This quality won commercial success too for his next film *Aux Yeux du Souvenir* also made in Hollywood style. Like Christian Jacque (*Sortilèges, Boule de Suif, La Chartreuse de Parme*), Delannoy is an honest craftsman, capable of good work and worthy of his international reputation. He committed a few mistakes, of which the most outstanding was *Les Jeux Sont Faits* with a bad script by the existentialist, Jean-Paul Sartre. The director Maurice Cloche, with the exception of *Monsieur Vincent*, seems unable to make a good film. *Monsieur Vincent*, a Catholic propaganda film, owes its success solely to the remarkable quality of Pierre Fresnay's interpretation.

All these films marked the summit of the careers of the directors concerned or else trod well-worn paths. It may be questioned, therefore, whether the French film has contributed any real or new advance since the war.

When speaking of the French contribution, it must be remembered that French film-making is still disorganized and disunited. A new post-war school as homogeneous as the pre-war school has not yet had a full chance of forming. But, perhaps, it is a lack of perspective in our contemplation which prevents us from seeing that these apparently isolated trees are planted in such an order and plan that they will produce a forest.

The months following the Liberation saw the revelation of a great film in *La Bataille du Rail*, and in René Clément, the director, the emergence of a strong personality. This Resistance picture of French railway workers far surpassed the documentary frame which had originally been meant for it. It really reached epic proportions in several of its episodes—the derailment of a German train, and the shooting of French railway workers by the Germans. The film equals in value the Swiss *The Last Chance* or Roberto Rossellini's famous *Rome, Open City*, although it is somewhat less in quality than the latter's *Paisa*. Completed a few months after the end of hostilities, *La Bataille du Rail* opened the way to a new 'French' realism comparable to what has since become Italian Neo-Realism. *Rome, Open City* by its huge success in the United States, and the large sums it earned there, set an example to Italian producers and proved a useful inspiration. The exhibition of *La Bataille du Rail* was limited to Continental Europe, including Russia, but the film was never exploited across the Atlantic.

These commercial facts injected a little strength into French production in spite of its timidity. The war was hardly finished when producers everywhere cried that the public was weary of war films. Some directors chorused that 'a certain perspective is indispensable to

118

the artist for treating an historical subject'. Facts belied this theory, however. Between 1945 and 1948 record box-office takings in Paris were recorded principally by war films. And the predominant quality of the Italian neo-realists lay in their ability to face contemporary history squarely.

In spite of the considerable success of *La Bataille du Rail* on the European market, the French cinema, except in a few rare cases, gave us war and Resistance subjects. There is little to say about Calef's *Jericho*, except that it did have moments of skill. Such music-hall vulgarities as his *Un Ami Viendra ce Soir* and *Les Clandestins*, which used a Resistance subject only as pretext, are better overlooked. During the years following the war, Jean Grémillon sought for months, without success, for a producer who would undertake his new film, *Massacre des Innocents*, which was a portrayal of seven years of European wars. Louis Daquin, without the means of making a contemporary subject, resigned himself to Sardou's old Victorian melodrama, *Patrie*, because the Occupation of Flanders during the seventeenth century had something in common with the recent Occupation in France, as was proved in a contrary sense in *La Kermesse Héroïque*. Christian Jacque, using the same parallel, adapted Maupassant's *Boule de Suif*, where the action is set in 1870.

In spite of this deficiency in production, the public wanted more films like *La Bataille du Rail*. To satisfy this demand, in 1948, a sound but uninspired documentary appeared called *La Bataille de l'Eau Lourde*, more Norwegian than French in origin, which turned out to be a great commercial success. Jean Dreville, who had collaborated with Titus Vibe Muhler, brought off a lively picture, *La Cage aux Rossignols*, with a story about children, that was very successful commercially. Then the author-actor, Noël-Noël, with René Clément made an amusing but too facile film, with a story of 'free and easy' Resistance—*Le Père Tranquille*.

In spite of the unofficial boycott on present-day events, René Clément managed to make another war subject, *Les Maudits*, an original story of a submarine filled with Nazis and collaborators, wandering about in the Atlantic after the fall of Berlin. Although the script was neither weak nor unconvincing, the film was dominated by the strong personality of the director. There were some remarkable scenes in the picture such as the hero's entry into the submarine, a final slaughter of madness and

119

fury, and an excellent transposition in mid-ocean of what was the end of Nazism in a Berlin in flames. But the commercial failure of this film forced Clément to abandon contemporary subjects and revive more hackneyed pre-war themes in his Franco-Italian *Au Delà des Grilles*. The brilliant technical qualities of this picture do not compensate for the banalities of a superficial script.

If the French cinema, like the Italian cinema, had courageously undertaken to portray recent history, such as the war and Resistance with its still bleeding wounds, it could have forged directly ahead. This sort of bold attitude would have eased its entry into the post-war era, as in Italy *Paisa* opened the path to *Bicycle Thieves*. The feeble withdrawal from immediate reality in French film-making hindered even directors with initiative and courage from taking up a decisive attitude. The post-war films following in the tradition of realism of the pre-war work of Renoir stopped apparently within the limits of a descriptive realism, little different from that to which they had been forced owing to the circumstances of Occupation.

From this point of view, the best example of French realism has been Jacques Becker's *Antoine et Antoinette*; it can be compared to *Le Crime de Monsieur Lange*, the latter typical of the period 1935-6. *Antoine et Antoinette* belonged essentially to 1947 in certain background details such as the ending of rationing difficulties. The film was both intimate and critical as the picture of the daily lives of the Parisian *bourgeoisie;* it had authenticity and was full of both charm and kindness in the best sense. But, unlike the best Italian films, nothing linked it to pressing post-war problems. It could well have dated from the old, joyous, carefree era of prosperity belonging to the time of René Clair's first films. If the search for a lost lottery ticket, which turned out to be the prize-winner, was more dramatic than the mad cavalcade in *Le Million*, this huge lottery prize produced far less in the way of social results than in *La Belle Equipe*.

Becker's work was not the less excellent because of this lack of weight. It did deserve the enthusiasm with which it was welcomed in France even if outside France certain of its traits were too specifically Parisian to be appreciated. From the technical point of view, the picture is characterized by a return of 'quick montage' and an almost complete absence of dialogue and anecdote, both of which are interesting and progressive tendencies. Jacques Becker did not achieve such satisfactory

120

results with *Rendez-Vous de Juillet*. The young people in this film, gyrating around colleges and hot-jazz clubs, were unaware of the serious problems of life; analysis and not description was needed to approach these problems. Consequently the film's interest is threadbare and diffuse, with the result that it lacks true significance.

Georges Rouquier's *Farrebique*, a contemporary of *La Bataille du Rail*, was both a curious and a strong piece of work. After having finished some interesting little films devoted to rural craftsmanship, *Le Charron* and *Le Tonnelier*, he was obviously inspired by the example of Flaherty's *Nanook of the North*, where an Eskimo family is transformed into actors and heroes. Flaherty had always limited himself to exotic lands, whether near or far. Contrary to his teacher, Rouquier found the subject matter for his film in his own family, living on a lonely farm in the Massif Central. The picture had lyrical passages of intense, gripping poetry, such as the death of the grandfather and the arrival of spring. Influences from the Soviet cinema were evident, but with this difference, that the picture remained simply and genuinely descriptive, with its world restricted to the narrow circle of the family and the farm. The relations of this family unit with the outside world were reduced to the minimum. The installation of electricity in the farmhouse is the central ambition of the family in *Farrebique*, but this detail, which is the only contemporary one, is a mere domestic problem. Nothing is said about the resources of these peasants; about their harvests, about the prices at which they buy or sell. This pre-occupation with triviality lessened the impact of Rouquier's remarkable work. After *Farrebique*, he would have liked to make more films on similar family themes, tales of Parisian workers or of the natives of North Africa. The chance did not arise; although *Farrebique* was a success, Rouquier has not made a film since.

The descriptive realism to which Becker and Rouquier limited themselves was, after all, the angle used in other less important works. Roger Leenhardt's *Les Dernières Vacances* was a sort of childhood diary, a sincere but often clumsy description of what the sale of a huge family estate represented for a southern landlord in 1925. *Paris 1900*, a picture made up of old newsreels, was a tribute to the courage, irony, wisdom and intelligence of the director, Nicole Védrès. Jean Gehret showed a robust sense of observation in his *Café du Cadran*, an almost anecdotal picture of daily life in a Parisian café-bar. The same quality was evident in his adaptations from André Chamson's peasant novels, *Tabusse* and

I

121

Le Crime des Justes. These pictures were shot almost entirely in the open, in the natural beauty of the Cevennes.

The tendency towards descriptive realism was often called intimate realism by some critics: perhaps the latter qualifying adjective is more correct. The common link between works as apparently diverse as *Farrebique* and *Antoine et Antoinette*, not to speak of the minor successes, is because they are conceived within the intimacy of a united family, with all the warmth of their daily joys and sorrows, without analysing exactly what binds this close, tiny world to its day and society. Perhaps the famous French individualism will revive through this quality of intimacy, so different from the spirit of *Le Ciel est à Vous*, in which Grémillon presented an heroic family as a general example.

Grémillon would doubtless have been the source of further inspiration for the French realist school had he been able to carry out his plans to make his film *Massacre des Innocents* or *Le Printemps de la Liberté*, with which he meant to commemorate the centenary of the 1848 revolution. True realism can be as well expressed in another epoch, even though far back in history, as in contemporary life. Instead of being able to carry out his own plans, however, Grémillon had to accept the job of directing *Pattes Blanches*, scripted by the dramatist, Jean Anouilh. Although temperamentally ill-suited to this assignment, Grémillon was able, through the medium of this conventional, tragic plot, to prove once again his marked talent for directing players. His sharp sense of reality was clearly evident in his description of a fishing village, which the obligations of the melodrama forced him to leave in the background.

Louis Daquin's *Le Point du Jour* appeared on the threshold of the half-century to strengthen the tendency maintained by Grémillon, René Clément, Becker, Rouquier, Leenhardt and, to some extent, the development started in *Les Portes de la Nuit* by Marcel Carné.

Le Point du Jour, devoted to the life of miners in the collieries of the North, although truly descriptive, can hardly be called intimate. Covering a vast canvas, it is a work which, in the background, poses urgent national problems. Vladimir Pozner's scenario needed a severe restraint of dialogue and action, such as de Sica was achieving at the same time in *Bicycle Thieves*. Daquin's work was, in the main, powerful and great, although it did not reach the level of perfect mastery. In the opening sequences, the rousing of the working districts and the men

122

going down into the mines was a great piece of 'cinema', unequalled in either French or German or English films dealing with mining life. For this alone *Le Point du Jour* was the best film made in 1949. It is not known yet whether the considerable perspective opened by this film will be followed by the French cinema of to-morrow. To rival the Italian cinema, French film-makers need to catch up with contemporary reality. The Italians made their big advance after learning, in the first place, from the French.

On the other hand, the French film of to-day has paved the way for future progress in other directions. A new direction has been set for comedy, a type of film which had almost faded out since 1914. The few isolated attempts made after 1930 which showed any promise were not followed up. The unequal series of *Ademai*, interpreted by the actor-author Noël-Noël must be mentioned. *L'Affaire est dans le Sac* directed by Pierre Prévert from a script by his brother Jacques, *Adieu Léonard* (1943) and then *Voyage Surprise* (1946) were worthy new attempts at French comedy by the Prévert brothers. The pervading tradition is the surrealism of the 'Cadavres exquis', with its baroque absurdity and humour. Also traceable is the American influence of Mack Sennett, Buster Keaton, Al Saint John and Harry Langdon. In *Adieu Léonard*, the optimistic, smiling presence of Charles Trenet does not fit in with Jacques Prévert's sombre sarcasm. The deliberately idiotic tone of *L'Affaire est dans le Sac* is exploited in many of the sequences. *Voyage Surprise* was more homogeneous, and renewed the old tradition of the chase, pursued through landscapes which are typically French. A rather forced liveliness spoilt this film, as was the case in *Le Couple Idéal*, with Raymond Rouleau as producer and leading player. It nevertheless opened a way to be followed by some commercial successes (like *Le 89 Part en Vacances* and *Nous Irons à Paris*) and, up to a point, by the finest French comic film since the war, *Jour de Fête*. Its director and star, Jacques Tati, was unwise to stretch out the rather thin comedy plot, and not to lay more emphasis on the background of a typical French village. But the character he creates of the rural postman unquestionably has life; he is very near to instituting a type. When he imitates an American documentary, or when he comes to grips with his archaic bicycle, Jacques Tati, instinctively or not, unites the best traditions of the pre-war comedies, and to a lesser extent, those of the Chaplin slapsticks. The simple good-heartedness of *Jour de Fête* never excludes poetry, which is all the more attractive here for being spontaneous, unlike the contrived comedies by the Prévert brothers. France breeds excellent comedians such as Fernandel and Bourvil, but they are almost always wasted in mediocre, clownish parts. It is unusual to find Fernandel in a role worthy of his talent, as in *L'Armoire Volante*, written and produced by Carlo Rim. This attempt at macabre comedy has decided quality, and so has *Les Casse-Pieds*, in which Noël-Noël embellished his rather easy-going but kindly interpretation of a Montmartre song-writer with a series of ingenious tricks.

If France could find a leader and technician comparable to Grierson in Great Britain, her documentary school would assume some definite form. Around Jean Painlevé—who has made some of his best films since the war in *Le Vampire*, *Assassins d'Eau Douce*, and *Solutions Françaises* —an excellent group of scientific film directors continues the good work. André Michel translated the lyricism of Aragon in *La Rose et la Réséda* into beautiful photography. By searching in the anthologies of old engravings, Alexandre Mercanton made a remarkable historical film, *1948*. In *Goëmons*, Anik Bellon paints with poignant truth the dismal life of the unhappy inhabitants of certain Breton islets, and Cousteau discovered the romantic lyricism in the splendours of the undersea world in *Epaves* and *Autour d'un Récif*. In *Lueur*, Doctor Thevenard continued experiments of the former *avant-garde*, and Franju showed a cold, academic ferocity in *Le Sang des Bêtes*. But in post-war France, films on the visual arts were the most fertile and most promising documentary subjects.

Without a doubt, the remarkable productions by Luciano Emmer on the work of such artists as *Giotto* and *Bosch* have exercised an influence on this type of film, but the Italian productions were still unknown during the Occupation when Lucot directed his intelligent film *Rodin* and Jean Lods, in his very remarkable *Maillot*, showed the great sculptor in his daily life at home among his native Pyrenees. These striking productions gave a particular quality to the French school, which insists on the humanity of the artists rather than on using their works to build up legends. Among the many varied films that emerged from this fruitful school of film-making was *Aubusson* by Jean Lods, *Matisse* by Campeaux —particularly notable for the astonishing penetration into the very thought of the artist through use of a slow-motion camera technique— *Images Médiévales* by Novik and especially *Van Gogh* by Alain Resnais, who won the 1950 Oscar for this documentary. But the same artist's *Guernica* surpasses this famous film, where the life of 'the man with the cut ear' is told rather in the fashion of an anecdote. The very beautiful poem by Eluard to Spain and the war is the basis of the dramatic subject matter of *Guernica* as depicted in Picasso's famous painting.

French cartoons, degenerate since the days of Emile Cohl, are enjoying a certain renaissance. Paul Grimault is now the leading master. He started before the war with publicity films of which one, in particular, *Les Lampes Mazda*, was admirable in its invention and fantasy. The war interrupted his full-length film *Les Passagers de la Grande Ourse*, which was shown only in an abridged and very mutilated version. His short films *L'Epouvantail* and *Le Voleur de Paratonnerres* have an original and intimate style, but the comedy remains on the intellectual level of a private joke. *Le Petit Soldat*, a tragic cartoon on war, is Grimault's masterpiece. It offered a hopeful prospect for his succeeding production, *La Bergère et le Ramoneur*. Grimault cannot be blamed for his spasmodic production, since the making of cartoon films in France is both difficult and unrewarding. The same lack of resource paralyses the scope of all short film production, which partly explains why a country with so many first-rate documentary makers lacks a documentary school.

What will be the future of the French film in the second half of the century? It began under happy auspices with René Clair's *La Beauté du Diable*, a modern Faust in which Man and the People conquer Destiny. But this great French film was made in Italy. As for *La Marie du Port*, Carné had to submit to such repressive conditions that his theme suffered even more than his technique. The French cinema doubtless possesses many hopes, such as Melville, who, in *Le Silence de la Mer*, proved himself a scrupulous technician, and Le Chanois or Jean Devaivre. But will they be given a fair chance? If the cancellation of the Blum-Byrnes agreements won certain economic advantages for the industry, these are now threatened in turn by a new and growing financial crisis.

The destiny of the art of the French film is linked to that of a nation which, in spite of the results of a devastating war, keeps a key position in the forefront of Europe's film-makers. If France wants to maintain the enviable position she won after 1930, she can no longer rest on these hard-earned laurels. She must strike out for further progress.

125

The prospect for the French cinema is not entirely happy, it desperately needs confidence in its own future. Only too often the industry has lost its front-rank men, just as the Swedish cinema did after the departure of Stiller and Sjostrom, when it was left headless and bloodless. But every decline, or hesitation, has been followed by a new upward surge. Let us hope, therefore, that we shall see, after 1950 as after 1935, the French Cinema carried forward by an enthusiasm which is backed by the whole nation.

INDEX

128

129